Praise for James Donaldson and *Celebrating Your Gift of Life*

"James Donaldson showed strength, determination, and endurance throughout his NBA career. I've watched him use these same attributes to persevere through business disappointments, health challenges, and especially bouts of depression. He has much to share on winning in the game of life."

— Eve Allen, PhD, Speaker, Author, and Wellness Consultant

"When I think of James, a PAC-10 student athlete, an NBA teammate, an NBA All Star, and someone with political aspirations who has traveled the world, the term 'gentle giant' comes to mind, not just because of his physical size but for his mental and worldly skills as well. James has always stood above the crowd, but he will always bend to take a stand and lend a hand to help. James, continue the journey of success and growth you stand for!"

— Lafayette "Fat" Lever, Teammate, Businessman,
Philanthropist, and Friend

"I first met James while he was playing for the Seattle SuperSonics. I was immediately struck by his tenacity on the court, and his kindness off. He is a complex, authentic, intelligent man whose disarming smile has often hid his inner struggles. James' courage to share his journey with mental illness will certainly benefit others, and his leadership to improve the human condition makes him a first ballot Hall of Famer."

— Keith Shipman, President & CEO, Washington State
Association of Broadcasters, Sportscaster, KOMO-AM/TV
Seattle (1983-85) and KCPQ-TV Seattle (1986-1999)

"I've known James Donaldson since 1975 when we first met in the sports weight room at Washington State University. He was a freshman basketball player and I was just getting started as a football player. It was obvious from day one that he was going to be a huge success. He had a burning desire to succeed and everyone knew it. His work ethic, along with his very sharp intellect, helped him transform his body from that of a gangly, skinny-framed freshman to an intimidating force by his senior year. As everyone knows, James went on to have a magnificent fourteen-year career in the NBA and in professional leagues across Europe. James has always been a leader, on and off the basketball court, and his new book, *Celebrating Your Gift of Life*, shows he is uniquely qualified to help many suffering from the terrible disease of depression. Despite his illustrious basketball career, James has battled many challenges, including depression, and now he wants to help others "find the light" in overcoming their major setbacks and challenges."

— Jack Thompson, Former Collegiate and NFL Player

"I've known James for more than twenty years, and he is totally qualified to write on the subject of mental health awareness. His writing is strong and direct. Through James' efforts, I've learned to take mental health issues more seriously, and I hope many lives will be saved through James' good work."

— Timothy Johnson, Tacoma, Washington

"James has been a close personal friend of mine for about seventeen years. Two of his qualities that have always impressed me are his optimism and goal-oriented nature. James is one of the most well-read people I've known, helped by his listening to audiobooks at 3x speed. He has always been fascinated by the study of human behavior, never guessing that a cascade of events would lead him to experience severe depression. His openness in sharing his journey will inspire all who read his book."

— Karen Koehler, Attorney, Seattle, Washington

"James has faced his challenges with strength and courage. His story can help others dealing with strife to face their challenges with the same courage he has. I highly recommend reading his book."

— Joseph Patrick McGivney, President of JP McGivney Company and President of JJC Ventures Corp

"I have known James Donaldson for a number of years. He is a caring and helpful individual and a positive force in educating people about mental health issues. I strongly support his efforts in this endeavor."

— Jeffrey Wysong, Commercial Real Estate Investor

"James is literally the big brother everyone wants to have. You feel safe and protected when he is around. In his books, he never preaches. He simply shares his feelings, feelings that everyone has, including his vulnerability. This makes it real and give us hope."

— David F. Chan, Fire Commissioner of South County Fire

"It takes a big man to admit he has little to live for. At 7' 2", James Donaldson is a towering figure of strength for sharing his story of surviving the depths of depression and the onerous emotional trail that led to his recovery."

— David Levy, Neighbor and Friend

"James, you have no idea how much I have enjoyed developing a great partnership with you in our CBD business as we've helped people explore the quality and benefits of CBD from hemp for our physical and mental health, happiness, and overall wellbeing. Your friendship continues to be a treasure and I look forward to many years ahead."

— Liz Diehl, Certified in CBD, Physiology, and Health

"When I met James, he was in deep distress and on the edge, ready to go over the cliff. I shared with him my own story. (Everything I had worked for gone in one day, POOF!) James was falling and did not know where to turn. Little did he know he was falling into Grace, and it was God's grace that put him back on his feet."

— Warren Mach, Senior VP, Davidson Wealth Management, LLC

"It takes a big man to publicly reveal his personal scars. James Donaldson's story is a penetrating reminder to seek help before imploding under the weight of life's cares. Confined emotionally to a 'dark and scary place,' he discovered enough light to appreciate God's amazing gift of life."

— George Toles, Seattle SuperSonics' Courtside Announcer
(1967-1986) and Former Team Chaplain

"Throughout our decades of friendship, James has often reached out to me and other friends to share his many success stories. But his life-saving outreach came about when he developed a friend's support action plan, which he used to help save his own life. During his darkest hours, suicidal thoughts were his constant companion. James' life was saved when he reached out to us in order to replace his 'constant companion.' When James did so, his friends were able to help him connect with his inner strengths, which he then used to fight off his demons. James utilized his friends as a major resource, and now today, he is employing his life-and-death story to help others choose life over death. I (and an unknown number of others) am greatly thankful that James chose life over 'the forever decision' of suicide."

— Chuck Wright MA, Washington State Licensed Mental Health Professional with Certification in Traumatic Stress

"To get through the dark times, James learned how to open up to the Love and Grace that surrounded him. Love and Grace that brightened his heart. Love and Grace so powerful that he has dedicated his life to lending his hand to help others who struggle. Read this to find your way. Read this to shine the way."

— Lisa Stuebing, Medical Exercise Specialist, Journalist, and Public Speaker

"James Donaldson is a big man who has endured big problems. Through a series of losses, he came to know despair, depression, and suicide, but he also developed a step-by-step process to pull him out of the depths and back into a meaningful and celebratory life. *Celebrating Your Gift of Life* is his gift to us."

— Tyler R. Tichelaar, PhD and Award-Winning Author of *Narrow Lives* and *The Best Place*

"James, I've known you for many years since I'm a huge basketball fan. We're from the same town of Sacramento and I've always been proud of you being from my hometown. Until I met you at Mrs. North's Celebration of Life, I had no idea what darkness you had just come through. Now I admire you even more than ever. My brother, Victor, also a collegiate basketball player, was in a similar dark place, for thirty-plus years. It was tough on family and friends. But it was torturous for him. He suffered from manic depression and homelessness from time to time, eventually leading to poor health and death. What you have been through is what many are struggling with, young and old. I believe God has brought you through this to show others that they are not alone. And to remind each of us that we need each other's help. Shine bright and remind us that we all affect each other."

— Dusty Baker, American Major League Baseball Manager, Current Manager of Houston Astros

"James Donaldson proves once more that we are in charge of our destinies. Although it seemed like Fate was against him as his world began to crumble around him, he made the choices necessary to get the help he needed and get back to his A-game. In *Celebrating Your Gift of Life*, he will show you how you can do the same, no matter what obstacles and hardships you face."

— Patrick Snow, Publishing Coach and International Best-Selling Author of *Creating Your Own Destiny* and *Boy Entrepreneur*

"Congratulations to James Donaldson on his excellent new memoir. James' book addresses the elephant in the room: mental illness that can accompany physical illness and major life events. James faced a life-threatening cardiac illness and battled his way back to excellent physical health. After his recovery, the dark specter of depression came upon him unexpectedly. He didn't run away, and he didn't try to hide his struggle from his physicians and friends. He was open, honest, and forthcoming about the issues he was facing. He faced the challenge head on and found a way through to recovery. Now, James shares his personal experiences with others so that they can recognize the warning signs of depression and mental illness and know that they don't have to suffer alone or choose drastic solutions to solve problems. The first and biggest challenge is to talk openly about it, and then to work collaboratively with healthcare professionals to address mental illness. It is my privilege to serve on James' healthcare team and support him in his endeavor to educate society about mental illness."

— Dr. Peter Casterella, MD, Cardiologist

"James came to see me at the very depths of his depression and anxiety. Together, we developed a recovery plan for him that included mental health counseling and pharmacological support. He made it through this very difficult time because he realized he needed help, reached out for medical support, followed through on the plan, and surrounded himself with a close group of intimate friends who were there for him every step of the way. After twelve months of hard work, he emerged from that darkness and began a new chapter in his life. There truly is a 'bright side' after the darkness. He found it, and you can too."

— Matthew Max Noell, MD

"In *Celebrating Your Gift of Life*, NBA All-Star James Donaldson shares hard truths about life and how disappointment and problems will come your way no matter how successful you are. Even though he was on the verge of suicide, James learned how to turn his life around, and now he shares his hard-earned wisdom with us all so we can understand what a gift life is, no matter what comes your way."

— Nicole Gabriel, Author of *Finding Your Inner Truth* and *Stepping Into Your Becoming*

An NBA All-Star Opens Up About His Mental Health Journey

CELEBRATING YOUR GIFT OF LIFE

FROM THE VERGE OF SUICIDE TO A LIFE OF PURPOSE AND JOY

JAMES DONALDSON

"No one is immune to the trials and tribulations of life. No one. We all have ups and we all have downs. That's just life."

— Martin Lawrence, Comedian

"Even though I walk through the valley of the shadow of death (darkness), I will fear no evil, for You are with me; Your rod and Your staff, they comfort me."

— Psalm 23:4

To Coach George Raveling and Coach Lenny Wilkens.

Thank you for always being there for me, both on and, more importantly, off the court.

SPECIAL THANKS

This book would not have been possible without the support of some special people:

Rosemary Bennetts—my long-time operations manager, who was the first person to reach out to check on me to see if I was okay.

Lisa Renee Brown—a true friend if there was ever one, who continues to encourage me to stay strong and hang in there.

Karen Koehler—she has continually showed me the true meaning of love and friendship.

Laura Vannucci—she somehow always found time to check in on me even though her own personal plate continually "overflows" with the love she shows for everyone.

Chuck Wright—he was able to help me see the "clinical" side of what I was going through, along with providing a wonderful friendship.

George Toles—he always encouraged me and reminded me that God has something even greater planned.

Antoinette Bryant—she demonstrated that she cared for me, even when I could care less about myself. A true friend.

Matthew Noell, MD—my family physician who took time with me as his patient to understand what I was going through and diagnosed my depression, anxiety, and suicidal ideations. Thank goodness he did!

Peter Casterella, MD—my cardiologist who was so compassionate and understanding of what I was going through, every step of the way.

Samuel Youssef, MD—my cardiac surgeon who became a dear friend. Thanks, Dr. Youssef. I owe you my life.

Sherrie Chatzkel—a dear friend who helped me to select this book's cover design.

CONTENTS

Foreword by Dr. Samuel Youssef   25

Introduction   29

Chapter 1   Growing Up   33

Chapter 2   How to Help Those in Need   39

Chapter 3   Sometimes You Get Kicked, Even When   49
             You're Down

Chapter 4   My Sham Marriage   59

Chapter 5   My Support Group   71

Chapter 6   A Moment of Reflection   79

Chapter 7   If I'd Gone Through With It   85

Chapter 8   God Is So Real to Me   93

Chapter 9   Find a Reason to Keep Living   97

Chapter 10   Working Your Way Back to Your Old   103
             Self

Chapter 11   Get Back in Touch With Yourself and   109
             Those Around You

Chapter 12   Keeping Agreements With Yourself   115

Chapter 13   Where Do I Go from Here?   127

Chapter 14   I'm So Glad I Didn't Sneeze   135

Chapter 15   I'm Not a Victim   139

Chapter 16   Learning Not to Act Needy   145

Chapter 17   I'm So Glad I'm Not an Angry Person   155

Chapter 18   Turning the Page   157

Chapter 19   Will Suicide Always Be an Option?   175

Chapter 20 I   Am Not a Victim, and Neither Are You   179

Chapter 21   How Do You Know When You've Hit Rock Bottom…and Does It Matter?   183

Final Thoughts   189

About the Author   193

Book James Donaldson to Speak at Your Next Event   195

FOREWORD

by Dr. Samuel Youssef

On that day, January 3, 2015, when James arrived via ambulance to the operating room at Swedish Hospital—Cherry Hill Campus, our surgical team went to work immediately to perform the surgery that had to be done right then and there to save his life.

As I held James' heart, literally, in my hand, I sensed then that he had a heart of gold, one that always thought of others before himself, that gave back, and that led by example.

Shortly after James' recovery, during one of his follow-up appointments with me, we walked the hospital intensive care unit floor where he had been a patient not so long ago. He gladly visited with several patients who were recovering from the same surgery he had undergone. He talked with them and encouraged and reminded them that they could, and would, recover, just as he had.

James showed me then just how much he cared.

A year or two later, James went through a serious bout of depression, anxiety, and suicidal ideations (not totally uncommon for patients who have gone through a life-threatening heart surgery like he had). He did the right thing in reaching out to his medical providers to assess what was going on and receive treatment to help work his way through all of it.

After twelve months of finding himself in that dark and depressed state, James felt the darkness start to lift. Then he realized he had a story to share and a life to live, so he began his "next chapter" of being an advocate and voice for mental health awareness and suicide prevention. He went on to establish his nonprofit, Your Gift of Life Foundation.

In this book, James recounts his experiences of having to work his way back to fully functioning and feeling like his old self. He also gives helpful advice to the reader to work their way through mental health issues.

Life is going to be filled with ups and downs and unexpected turns.

James' story reminds us all that there is a bright side somewhere…and we shouldn't stop until we find it.

It's there for all of us.

Dr. Samuel Youssef, MD
Cardiac Surgeon
Swedish Hospital, Seattle, Washington

INTRODUCTION

Needless to say, choosing suicide would have been the most foolish, regrettable, and outright stupid decision I could have ever made.

I understand that when someone is in that dark and scary place, there seems to be no hope and no tomorrow. I was there. Not only did I feel there was no hope and no tomorrow, but I also felt like the scum of the earth; I felt disappointed with myself, like an utter failure, and like I was totally worthless. So I know of what I speak. This book is about how I was able, with God's Grace, to hang in there even on those days when I felt I had nothing to hang on to. It is about how I was able to realize something was wrong and reach out for professional medical help and to a group of intimate, caring, and loving friends.

If you ever find yourself in this painful place, please, I beg of you, don't end your life. As is often said, "Suicide is a permanent solution to a temporary problem." I know when you're in that dark place, your problems seem permanent, like you can never get through them, but believe me, you have to allow yourself to be helped, and you must allow yourself to feel the love and caring of the many people around you who truly do care about you. They cared about me. With professional help, medication, and support from friends and family, I was able to lift myself up out of depression and suicidal thoughts. This book tells that story.

James Donaldson

James Donaldson

Chapter 1

GROWING UP

Until January 2015, I lived what many people would consider a charmed life. With determination and hard work, I seemed to have achieved just about everything I set out to achieve.

My first sense of real accomplishment came when I graduated from Luther Burbank High School in Sacramento, California, in 1975. From there, it was on to Washington State University in Pullman, Washington (1,100 miles north of Sacramento). I graduated from Washington State University in 1979.

During those developmental years, I had a lot of great mentors and coaches along the way to whom I felt accountable, which helped me be accountable to myself.

From Washington State University, I took a slight detour before I was able to get into the NBA, but I welcomed that detour by playing professional basketball in Siena, Italy (1979–1980). This decision really gave me a chance to spread my wings. I became very independent and learned about the world around me. Living in another country, learning another language, and making friends (who are still my friends today) was an education I just can't put a price tag on. Sure, I went to Italy kicking and screaming because I wanted to play in the NBA, but I didn't know what was best for me; it turned out my coaches and my agent knew better, so they recommended a year of seasoning myself playing professional basketball full-time in Italy; that was better than sitting on a bench in the NBA and never getting the chance to play, or worse, being cut early, so I would never be able to develop a full-fledged career.

After I returned from Italy, I tried out with the World Champion Seattle SuperSonics. It was a long shot for me to make the team, but my coach, Hall-of-Famer Lenny Wilkens, saw enough potential to keep me on the team, even though I was one of the last guys sitting on the bench. I was able to practice every day and get myself "NBA ready." I made it through my rookie year before breaking into the starting lineup playing alongside some great veteran teammates, including Jack Sikma, Lonnie Shelton, John "JJ" Johnson, Wally Walker, Fred "Downtown" Brown, and Gus "the Wizard" Williams. It was a great team for me to break in with. Two of the old veterans, Fred Brown and John Johnson, used to meet me before practice and keep me late after practice. We would work on rebounding drills, playing with my back to the basket, and slowly developing me into an NBA player. I give those guys so much credit for taking me under their wings to help me get started and ensure I developed the right way.

My NBA career ended up lasting fourteen years, with an All-Star appearance in 1988 when I was playing with the Dallas Mavericks. I can truthfully say I loved every moment of it. I don't think I ever had a bad day, even when I came crumbling down on the basketball court in The Summit in Houston, Texas, during one of our NBA games in 1989. That day, I suffered a ruptured patella tendon. It was career-threatening because by then I was considered an older player at thirty-two. But even then, I had a determined optimism that drove me to do all the physical therapy exercises, strength training, make a total recovery, returning to the basketball court the very next season. It was "a miracle of miracles," and I think a lot of it had to do with my overall mindset and attitude.

QUESTIONS FOR REFLECTION

What difficult situation are you confronting right now?

_____

_____

_____

What is a previous difficult situation you went through, and how did you get through it?

_____

_____

_____

What did you learn from that situation that you could now apply to your current situation to help you get through it?

_____

_____

_____

Chapter 2

HOW TO HELP THOSE IN NEED

This chapter is about what to do if you need help. In the last year, many people have shared their experiences with me, detailing their depression and anxiety and their suicidal thoughts. Often, the people I would have least expected were the ones dealing with these issues. They kept their pain from the rest of the world and dealt with it the best they could. Many people still deal with these issues in isolation. When we think about it, how well do we really know our neighbors? Do we really know our colleagues and coworkers? And when it comes down to it, do we really even know our significant other as well as we think we do? If we really start digging below the surface, we discover there are quite a few things we don't know about those closest to us.

I found that out for myself in February 2019, during a big snowstorm in Seattle. If you know Seattle, then you know when it gets hit with four or five inches of snow, the whole city can be paralyzed for a week. This snowstorm deposited six inches of snow on the first day, and three or four more the next. It stayed on the ground for quite a while, meaning that navigating the streets and the neighborhoods was tricky.

Needless to say, schools had a snow day. One of my dear friends, who lives by the airport, teaches at a middle school nearby. She was off work when the snow arrived on Friday, with more on Saturday and Sunday, and still more Monday and Tuesday. So she was stuck in her apartment alone (except for her little dog) and felt the walls were closing in. At the time, she was involved in some negative family dynamics, pertaining especially to her two adult children and her grand-children. She had raised her children in a fundamentalist household. When her kids moved out and found life partners, their partners weren't as firm in their religious convictions as their mother was. The mother thought everything would be fine because, eventually, the kids would return to their re-ligious upbringing. Well, the kids actually got further away from it, causing a divide between them and their mother. At the time of the snowstorm, the mom hadn't spoken to her son in at least five years. The daughter lived overseas and had re-cently blocked her mother from her Facebook and Instagram profiles. That really sent the mother over the edge.

So, during this five-day period, I was on the phone with my friend for three or four hours a day trying to talk her back from the edge of suicide. She kept saying, "After all the love I gave my children, this is how they treat me." She couldn't understand why she was no longer a priority in their lives. She couldn't understand why she was no longer able to inter-act with her grandchildren either. She started asking, "Where is God?" She had remained a pretty firm believer, but now was having doubts about whether God was real. Wondering where God was in her time of crisis began to cloud her mind and affect her judgment. After three or four days of listening to her 90 percent of the time, and only once in while trying to inject a little wisdom, I finally thought, *I've done all I can do to help her.* Of course, she was my friend, so I cared about her and didn't want harm to come her way, but I didn't see how I could help her further.

About this time, I was working with my friend, Chuck Wright, who has provided mental health therapy for clients in my physical therapy business for quite a few years. I shared with Chuck my friend's situation. He suggested that since she didn't want to see a counselor or anyone who could help her or have any visitors, that I should call the police in her neighborhood to go do a "wellness call." The police went and knocked on her door. After answering a couple of simple questions, in which she indicated she was fine and everything was okay, the police checked with a couple of her neighbors to ensure she was okay.

Once the police left, my friend, who sensed that I had made the call, turned on me with a vengeance. I knew she was not in her right mind at this point and didn't really know exactly what she was doing or saying. She essentially ended our friendship, telling me, "This is why I don't let people know what's going on with me." This was exactly the wrong reaction because times of darkness and despair are when we most need people to check in on us and let us know we are still loved.

A year prior, I had been in the exact same situation, going

through the same kind of pain. During a consultation with one of my doctors, who was sitting only a couple of feet away, my doctor reached out toward me and said, "Hey, James, if you take your life, so many people are going to miss you, and so many people are not going to understand. So many people care for you. So many people love you." I took those words in, but I couldn't connect with any of them. I looked right back at him and said, "Doc, nobody's going to miss me; nobody cares about me; nobody's going to be disappointed." That's exactly how I felt. That's why, when we are in those deep, dark places, we have to have sense enough to trust a friend or someone who cares about us to help guide us through. The toughest thing is going through it alone.

It is particularly difficult for men to speak up, reach out, and show weakness by letting people know exactly what they are going through. A lot of men I've talked to won't even tell their spouses what's going on; they might say things or behave in ways that are out of character, but they don't share what's going on. That leaves the spouse in the awkward position of knowing something is not quite right, but not to what extent. So, men, I really encourage you to reach out. Find a support buddy who can be there for you at all times. Find someone with whom you can let your hair down, talk with over a drink or coffee, and just really open yourself up to by being vulnerable so they can help you. That's how I made it through.

I continue to think calling the police was the right thing to do for my friend. She may be mad at me, and hate me now, but I have a feeling that somewhere down the road, when the fog and the clouds of despair lift, she'll look around and realize I was, indeed, a true friend to her and only looking out for her wellbeing.

I want to share another incident involving one of my doctors who I see twice annually. When I shared with him what I'd been going through, he was very sympathetic. He told me two or three doctors at his hospital had committed suicide recently. Each time that happens, everything is all hush-hush because people don't know what to say or do. The medical profession has one of the highest rates of suicide because of all the stress they endure, from days jam-packed with patients they can't spend enough time with to constant paperwork and the occasional surgery or patient recovery that just doesn't go as hoped.

This doctor and I made a pledge to each other to always be there for each other no matter what. I was seeing him in some of my darkest and most desperate days, and he knew it and really felt for me.

Well, when I recently went to see him, he just looked horrible—unkempt, with his clothes just hanging off him because he had lost a lot of weight. When I mentioned his weight loss, he acknowledged it and told me he just wasn't sleeping at night.

Right away, I could sense something was wrong. Of course, in the office, he was trying to put on a brave face, trying to keep his personal problems from affecting his professional life. I called him at home that evening to make sure he knew

I was thinking about him and that I was there for him. He mentioned a couple of nurses in his office were worried about him. He told me his stress was all work-related. There had been a big change in hospital management that was causing a lot of stress for a lot of folks. Even though he's a specialist at the top of his field, stress can get anyone, no matter who they are. That night, I talked to him for a good half hour to reassure myself he would be okay and not harm himself and to give him a breather. Then I wished him a good night's sleep.

I followed up with him for the next few days, with a phone call or a text message, sometimes with an inspirational quote just to give him a lift and good start to his day. I let him know he's important, loved, and matters.

Those are the things we tend to forget when we are in those deep, dark, desperate places.

When trying to support another, it's best not to act like you have all the answers or be judgmental—just be a friend with an attentive ear. That's what we all need the most during times of duress and stress that we just don't think we can handle anymore.

Those are some the things we can do, and we have to do, when someone reaches out to us in desperation. Offer them help. Also, since my teacher friend and I are both really strong Christians, I constantly reminded her of God's love for us. I reminded her that God would not want us to end this gift of life we are given. And I told her God is there, even when it doesn't seem like it. Even in my darkest days, when I was totally and absolutely alone, I knew one thing for sure: God was still with me. Of course, I didn't understand why God was letting me go through these things; I think that's where my anger came from. Sometimes we don't have the same understanding God does. But now that I've gone through that difficult time, I realize why God left me here—why God gave me just enough courage and encouragement to hang on. God did it because I would have a story to tell and share with people around the world. God did it because people look at me as a big physical specimen of a human being, strong and powerful, tall and athletic, and yet they will see that all of this happened to me, and that it just broke me down to being a babbling baby sometimes. He left me here to let men know "it's okay not to be okay." There's no shame in that game, and we men, who have, for the most part, been brought up not to cry or show weakness, need to realize when something is not quite right with us, and to allow ourselves to reach out for help and support. God left me here to tell my story so I can continue reaching out to our young people, letting them know there is hope, letting them know there will be a tomorrow, and that people do care about and love them, even if they can't feel it right now. That realization will be there as soon as the veils of darkness lift a little. It took me nearly eight months before the darkness started lifting for me. Before I finally started seeing that, yes, there is a future filled with wonderful opportunities directly ahead for me. It may not be exactly what I wanted, but it will be there.

I add that it wasn't exactly what I wanted because I wanted to continue to be a business owner, heading my team of employees as we worked on the great things we were doing. But God had other plans for me. Even though that business crashed and burned, I have been able to rise out of the ashes. I have become someone who can really go out and make a difference, hopefully, to thousands upon thousands of people, but even if I only make a difference to one, that will be joy divine.

QUESTIONS FOR REFLECTION

Name someone who has helped you through difficult times in the past. What did you learn from that experience that you can apply to your present experience?

_____

_____

_____

Sometimes by helping others, we can better help ourselves. Is there anyone who is hurting right now you can reach out to? If so, reach out to them now and write down how you felt after doing so.

_____

_____

_____

Make a list of at least five people you might consider asking to be your check-in buddy. After making your list, pick the person you feel most comfortable talking to. Ask them if they would like to be part of your two-person team of mutual support.

_____

_____

_____

Chapter 3

SOMETIMES YOU GET KICKED, EVEN WHEN YOU'RE DOWN

"If you haven't been through challenging times yet,
then just keep on living."

— Rev. Samuel Barry McKinney[1]

In 2018, several times I thought to myself, *I don't know how much more I can take.*

One such time was in June of that year. I went into the hospital for an arterial bypass operation as part of a procedural follow-up to the aortic dissection surgery I'd had three years earlier. It was supposed to be a relatively simple procedure compared to what I'd been through so far. They were going to make a large incision in my neck to reach my chest cavity; then, with some plastic bypass tubing, they would create an artificial bypass to increase blood flow to my brain so I would no longer suffer the

---

1 Rev. McKinney was my pastor at Mount Zion Baptist Church for nearly thirty years. He lived to the ripe old age of ninety-one, and even though he was wheelchair-bound and in assisted living, he was otherwise the picture of health with a sharp mind until the end.

lightheaded, dizzy sensations that had plagued me the previous two or three years. Well, this seemingly simple operation back-fired. Less than twenty-four hours after the bypass material was inserted, I developed a severe infection that made my neck swell up grotesquely, and I experienced a tremendous pressure in my chest cavity. Consequently, my projected twenty-four-hour hos-pital stay became a weeklong ordeal. As a former top-flight ath-lete, I'm used to being big and strong and physically able to do just about anything I want to do. Since my aortic dissection surgery in January 2015, that has been far from the case and many times, a cause of emotional turmoil. There I was, remem-bering how I physically did things just a short while before, and all of a sudden, I was having difficulty even walking up a flight of stairs or walking across a grocery store parking lot. Muscle fatigue would set in quickly, and my breathing would become short, so it was very challenging for me. So, I dealt with it all. I had surgeries in 2015, 2016, we thought we had finally fixed the problem in 2018. And yet another surgery in 2020 for a partial-ly paralyzed right lung that was collapsing upon itself and was only 1/3 of the size it should have been, thus causing an ongoing shortness of breath for even the slightest exertion.

Well, the infection from this latest procedure was very, very serious, requiring several days of intravenous antibiotics in the hospital, and then they put me on oral antibiotics for the next six months. During this time, I really felt the antibiotics' after-ef-fects. I felt very lethargic and easily fatigued; my joints had lots of aches and pains, and every step I took reminded me my mus-cles seemed to be chronically sore. This situation went on for two or three weeks before we finally discontinued the antibiotics and crossed our fingers. My infectious disease doctor told me if the infection came back, it would be "catastrophic and potentially life-threatening." Those words really got my attention, so I followed every step of his instructions to ensure I would get better. Finally, after nearly six months, the surgical site healed and I started to feel more like myself. It had been a long ordeal.

In July that year, while I was sitting in my hospital room, I got a notice from the National Basketball Retired Players Association (NBRPA). I was a long-standing (always in good standing) board member, but now the other board members, against all policy, procedures, and bylaws, were planning to vote on removing me from the board. I tried to push back the best I could from my hospital bed by letting them know I was in no position to attend any conference calls or even defend myself. I suggested a two-month leave from the board of directors, but the rest of the board ignored my request. I finally told them I could not make the scheduled conference call because I was in the hospital. They voted me off the board, which was a huge blow to me because I had given so much of my time, energy, and passion to helping our retired NBA players make the transition into life after basketball. I couldn't believe the board would do that to me, but I'd had several run-ins with various board members in the previous few months; those run-ins had all been related to personal and petty issues, and had little or nothing to do with my board service, but there were enough for my fellow board members to decide to gang up on me. They took the opportunity to kick me when I was down.

This situation with the board had begun in January when I decided to put my name in the hat as a candidate to become the NBRPA's executive director. The board didn't like this because they had their own handpicked candidate in mind, but anyone interested in the position was allowed to apply for it, even a board member. I had shown interest in this position in 2009 and received similar pushback from many of the same board members then. Much of the NBRPA's leadership has a serious lobster mentality: You're not going to reach the top of the barrel and get out of here because the rest of us will clamp down on you and bring you right back into the mess with us. It's pure envy and jealousy, professional jealousy. I don't think it's anything personal. They just didn't like that I didn't march in lockstep with them and vote exactly as they did on all the issues that came up. In the seven years I'd been on the board, I was always among those board members asking questions, demanding accountability and transparency, and not rubberstamping everything placed in front of me just to get along with everyone. I was there to assist players in their transition into retirement, not to line my pockets with any perks or benefits, as many of the board members do. I was there to be a voice for the retired players, to represent them at the board level, to suggest actual programs and activities that would be beneficial for them. The rest of the membership really appreciated that about me, but not the association's leadership.

When I interviewed for the executive director job, word went out that I didn't do good work: I didn't represent well; I didn't speak well; I didn't have any new ideas. The truth is, I was going into a pre-fabricated situation in which, as NBA management told me, "The NBA has already identified who they want to be their executive director for the retired players," and then I was told, "James, we want you to be okay with it." I wasn't okay with it, and they weren't okay with me not being okay with it, so they decided to get rid of me.

The NBRPA's leadership is made up of the executive director, the executive committee, which is composed of several committee chairs, and usually one or two other folks. The remainder is made up of the remaining board members. In the seven years I was on the board, information and the association's direction always came from those who were part of the executive committee (inner circle) who cozied right up to the executive director or to the NBA itself.

For the NBA, the NBRPA is one of their little throwaway programs to show they are doing something for retired players. The NBRPA was begun in 1992, by NBA hall of famers Dave DeBusschere, Dave Bing, Oscar Robertson, Dave Cowens, and Archie Clark. The intent was to try to get some benefits for players post-career.

In January 2017, the National Basketball Players Association (NBPA), an entirely different entity from the NBA itself, set out to provide healthcare coverage for every retired NBA player who is vested into the pension plan for at least three years. I qualified for that and then some with a premium package of healthcare coverage for myself and my family, and an increase in benefits. So that's the best thing that the NBA or the NBPA has ever done for the NBRPA or retired players. Other than that, we are "out of sight, out of mind" in the eyes of the NBA.

Few superstar players choose to hang around with the NBRPA

unless they can get their pockets lined with some perks or benefits. Superstars are typically under contract with the NBA, so the NBA can always call upon Larry Bird or Magic Johnson to make this or that appearance, pay them tens of thousands of dollars, and say they are working with retired players. That is so far from the truth. The NBA does provide the overall operating budget for the NBRPA—about $1,800,000 annually, of which about 60 percent goes toward overhead and the salaries and bonuses of the executive director and staff in Chicago. The rest of us are volunteers, including the chapter leaders. That's the NBRPA's overall makeup and structure. It's a horrible situation where we essentially sell our souls to the NBA for $1.8 million. In return, we agree to stay in this little organization and not do anything to generate any additional revenue (especially that involves any NBA licensure or merchandising) for ourselves or the NBRPA without the NBA's explicit approval. Of course, that's ripe with all kinds of caveats and everything else the NBA typically says no to.

I love all the players in the NBRPA, which includes retired NBA, ABA (American Basketball Association, which operated from 1967-1976 before being absorbed into the NBA), WNBA (Women's National Basketball Association), and the Harlem Globetrotters players. I love all of them because we've all been through a common experience. We all understand the struggles and challenges of trying to make a successful transition from playing to life after the game. I've done all I could to be as helpful as I possible to as many of the players as I could by working on scholarship opportunities for the retired players, revenue-generating opportunities that meet the approval of the NBA, etc.

Being terminated from the NBRPA board of directors felt like a sucker punch to the solar plexus that just doubles you over. But in a roundabout way, it gave me the incentive to ensure I move forward and do something even more rewarding with my life. I'm sure I can always circle back and do something with the NBRPA (as long as it's approved by the NBA), and I'm creating opportunities all the time to benefit individual players, such as mentoring opportunities between retired players and young players and international opportunities for retired players to work with basketball camps abroad. Meanwhile I have nothing but disdain and disrespect for the leadership of the NBRPA—it's hard to believe its board members and I once ran up and down the same court together—we should, if anything, epitomize what team play is all about. Teamwork is something that remains a part of a great team player throughout their athletic career, especially in a sport like basketball, where one player can really make a difference to the team.

Unfortunately, this experience has showed me that even though we all went through coaching with coaches who were leaders, it didn't teach us to be leaders ourselves. We were not taught to lead, only to follow. I honestly can't blame anyone but the players themselves for the plight of the NBRPA. All of us had the chance to make better lives for ourselves. Most of us made hundreds of thousands of dollars, many of us millions, during our playing careers. If we were smart, we figured out how to parlay that into living out our lives in luxury and ease. But most of us—I'd say 70 or 80 percent—found a way to spend all that money, get in debt, develop health issues because we didn't pay attention to our health, and find ourselves divorced, often two or three times, and paying child support. All these situations com-pounded will totally bankrupt just about anybody. That's the ex-perience of many retired players. Yes, we look and talk a good game; we all look so nice and tall and elegant, and some of us are well spoken, but truth be told, most of us are really struggling with various aspects of life. I feel for players in this situation, and I continue to be as supportive as I can, but I learned a long time ago that if I'm not welcome in particular circles, there's no need for me to bang my head against the wall. This is exactly the type of arrangement the NBA wants—a very dysfunctional group that can never get its act together to bring enough collec-tive clout to do or demand certain things. The NBA can treat us that way because we allow it to.

I'll continue to uncover opportunities for individual retired play-ers, whether here in the States or overseas in China where I spent a lot of time. Basketball is a fantastic game, and opportunities are all around us, but we have to be able to identify and cultivate them. Regardless, I will be all right with or without the NBRPA. I have a platinum membership, which is good for a lifetime, so good luck to them in trying to cancel that. I'm sure they won't push me down that road.

Both my situations with my health and with the NBRPA made me feel like I was being kicked when I was down. However, I used these situations as motivators more than anything to get myself up and keep on going. Even though they got me down, I have been able to bounce back and become better than ever. In fact, I'm light years ahead of where so many of my NBRPA colleagues are.

QUESTIONS FOR REFLECTION

Do you ever feel like if you do good, you end up paying for it? Describe a time when this happened.

_____

_____

_____

Have you experienced lobster mentality? Did you give in to it, letting it pull you down, or did you fight all the harder to achieve your goals?

_____

_____

_____

You can't win them all or make everyone like you. What have you learned or can you learn from situations where people unfairly turn against you?

_____

_____

_____

Chapter 4

MY SHAM MARRIAGE

One of the most stressful situations I dealt with in 2018 was coming to the realization that my marriage was nothing but a sham.

Let me take you back a little to 2011, when I met my now ex-wife on Match.com (International). At the time, she was in China, and I was in Seattle. I was doing a lot of work in China and anticipating it continuing for several years, which it did. My future wife and I communicated for a good eight or nine months over the phone, instant messaging, and sometime via Skype the best we could. She spoke virtually no English when I met her, but she was willing to learn. With the assistance of her aunt, who could speak just a little English and help with translation, we continued to communicate until I made a return trip to Beijing in October. She agreed to come down to Beijing where I was staying, along with her auntie, to meet me in person for the first time.

For me, it was love at first sight. Of course, I'd fallen in love with her over the internet, but meeting her in person really cemented it. Even though language was somewhat of a barrier, plenty of people and friends were around to help us communicate. It was quite the scene—me, this very large human being, seemingly out of place in mainland China, hanging out with a Chinese woman.

Culturally speaking, quite a few Chinese women secretly wish for the type of love affair we have in Western culture. In China, saying "I love you" and showing outward signs of affection, especially after marriage, is rare. I think many of the women are starving for love and affection, which they don't usually receive from their Chinese husbands. A lot of the marriages are marriages of convenience and practicality. There's more of a sense of "What can this person do for me, and what can I do for them?" compared to the love and euphoria we experience in the West. I had heard about these situations before, but now I was witnessing them firsthand living in China. I'd also heard stories where Chinese women, and international women in general, would want to get married to a foreigner to get a green card and citizenship to whichever country the man was from; then, shortly after getting a green card, they abruptly leave the marriage. Never, in my wildest dreams, did I ever imagine that could happen to me and my wife.

After we met in Beijing, we hung around for a month or two at the hotel before going to her hometown to be married in the province where she lived. It was no big deal, really, but basically an engagement ceremony; first, we went in front of a justice of the peace on December 25, 2011. After taking a few photos, we went back to my hotel where my new wife had arranged a reception for her family and friends to meet me. I and a staff member from the hotel were the only English-speaking people there, but we managed to make it through. We took a lot of great photos and were filmed together in videos. It was a great time with her family and all the kids and grandkids running around. My wife had a small son of about three when I first met her. I became very attached to him over the next several years. He was there, running around with the three or four other children present.

I had always, in my mind and my heart, planned, wanted, and thought I would marry someone I truly loved and who truly loved me. I didn't care about her status, background, culture, or even if she spoke English (as long as she was willing to learn English). I've learned how to communicate well with quite a few of my "English as a second language" friends throughout my life. So that was how we came together, and we ended up being married for five years until I filed for divorce in late 2017.

For the first couple of years of marriage, she and her little boy stayed in China while she continued to work and her son was looked after by his grandparents. That worked out fine because I went back and forth to China several times in 2012 and 2013.

Finally, just before the school year began in September 2013, she and her son moved to Seattle to be with me. Here we were, married in China, but still without any official ceremony or wedding in the United States. We never did get around to having a wedding or going before a justice of the peace in the United States to get any kind of marriage registration in place in America.

Once they were settled with me in Seattle, her little boy adapted tremendously well. All of a sudden, he had lots of American friends, who were kids up and down the street and at the neighborhood school he attended. He learned English quickly, as kids are apt to do. Within a few months, he was acting and almost talking like a little American boy—and also eating a lot of American food. It was a great time for me. I really felt like I finally had the family I had always dreamed of. I didn't have any children of my own, so my wife and I began thinking about having another child once we got settled in Seattle.

For the first year, I helped out quite a bit with the school to make sure the little boy adapted well to his teachers and counselors. I attended all the parent-teacher conferences while my wife kind of stayed away because she felt uncomfortable not being able to speak English very well. That was fine; I was more than willing to take on looking after his schooling. We got through the first year without any problems, and I felt like our marriage was really on solid ground. In 2014, I started the immigration paperwork for them. It was a long process, with a couple of steps forward and then a step back on occasion, but we were able to get most of it accomplished before I had major open-heart surgery in January 2015.

In Chinese culture, people don't really tend to have friends of the opposite sex they run around with. In America, we do that all the time. The vast majority of my life has been filled with platonic female friends. My wife didn't seem to understand this and thought it quite odd. When I was in the hospital for two months in January and February 2015, my hospital room became like Grand Central Station. I had so many friends coming by to check on me, and on occasion, a single female friend would come by to sit by my bedside and spend a little time with me. My wife thought this so strange that she suspected I might have something going on with all these women. She wasn't worried about the ones who came in with family members; she was more worried about the ones who were single and coming to see me by themselves. She was also very possessive and territorial toward the nurses who cleaned up after me, changed my bed linen, and performed other tasks she felt it was her place to do. She basically wanted all these women to stay away. Maybe it was a cultural thing, I never realized how insecure she was about our relationship until I was ready to be discharged.

Once I got out of the hospital, I spent the rest of 2015 having to take it easy, so I mostly just stayed around the house. My wife was great about taking care of my daily needs and accompanying me to my doctor appointments so she could learn exactly what was happening to me. She was also great about helping her son with his homework. I helped out quite a bit as well, making sure we had dinner on the table for the three of us every evening. All that went well. I continued doing what I would normally and naturally do as a responsible spouse. I made sure she was as comfortable as could be and engaged in the Seattle community. I found her a Chinese-speaking banker, Chinese-speaking life insurance agent, Chinese-speaking doctor, Chinese-speaking vet, Chinese-speaking attorneys—you name it. Everybody I brought into our lives spoke Chinese fluently so my wife could ask any questions she liked and have them answered in a language she was comfortable with to prevent any misunderstandings. I also had a lot of Chinese-speaking friends who would talk to her from time to time and try to help her understand American culture and how different it is from Chinese culture. I also helped her get a nice job in downtown Seattle at a prestigious private hotel and athletic club. I was thinking of buying her an economy car, but she insisted she really wanted a BMW, so I went ahead and found an affordable, used BMW—a cute little two-door sedan she had fun driving around. Chinese culture is very much into brand recognition, and BMW is a name they recognize right off the bat. I was looking at Hondas and Audis, but she really wanted a BMW. And it was totally fine with me; it was the first luxury car I've ever owned—and it was too small for me to drive.

Everything went well until about June 2017. Then I went out of town for a weekend golf tournament in Sacramento. When I came home Sunday evening, our house was eerily quiet and looked like it had been mostly vacated. I went looking around the house, but my wife and her son were nowhere to be found. The little boy's room had been cleaned out and all his clothes taken away. When I looked into our bedroom, the closet my wife and I shared was half empty—all her clothes and personal belongings were gone. She hadn't touched anything of mine; all my personal stuff was still there. She had just taken everything that was hers and her son's. She had also taken her car. Not until three or four days later did I get a text message from her—the only one—that she would bring the car back when she had finished moving. I had no idea where she went. I had no idea she was unhappy, and I had no idea this was something she had apparently been planning for a while. I was really confused because I didn't see any of this coming at me.

This incident sent me into a serious cycle of depression, anxiety, loneliness, and suicidal thoughts. For the rest of 2017, I came home to a big, empty house, void of the little boy's laughter and playing, void of her cooking great meals for us every evening, void of anybody sleeping next to me. Every day when I got home from running around Seattle, as soon as I sat down, the walls of the house started closing in on me. Here I was, alone and listening to a lot of the negative self-talk that goes on when you're in such a situation.

It was very sad, but somehow, I made it through the summer and early fall of 2017, until Thanksgiving approached. Then I was really at my very worst. I felt suicidal. Nothing seemed worth living for; every aspect of my life was upside down and over. My business was hanging on by a string, and I was spending my life savings trying to keep it afloat. My health was still iffy, so I could hardly do anything I used to. My mother died that same year, which was another big blow to deal with. I was undergoing an IRS audit of both my personal and corporate finances, which ultimately left me owing hundreds of thousands of dollars I'll never be able to repay. So, everything was upside down. I was hurting and hurting bad.

Yet in the midst of all that darkness, even when I was waking up at 1 or 2 a.m., I always knew God had a plan for me. God was allowing me to go through these things so I could have firsthand knowledge of what it's like for somebody in dire straits, feeling suicidal, and feeling devoid of hope. That was exactly where I was. At times, I seriously doubted I would make it through the holidays. Every day, every hour, was a struggle just to get through. It was a desperate time, and I was grasping for straws.

Finally, I realized something was definitely wrong with me and I needed help. I reached out to my family physician and began the process of getting the medical and personal care I needed. I also reached out to my close group of intimate friends to help me.

People asked me if I was angry with my ex-wife. I replied, "No, I'm not. I have a very forgiving heart." That was something a lot of my Chinese friends couldn't understand. Because I am a Christian and try to live how God would have me, I can forgive. I don't forget, but I can forgive. I won't go down that road again. In fact, I'm okay if I never see her again, though I do miss her son.

I don't feel bad toward the Chinese or their culture because of this incident. I realize one individual does not represent all the Chinese. I don't feel bad toward any immigrant woman who wants to come to this country. I don't feel bad toward women in general. I just know that next time I give my heart to someone, I'll be a lot more careful. I was lucky I didn't get burned more than I did. I don't think my wife knew anything about domestic law or the laws of separation here in the States, or if she did, maybe she didn't care. She never asked me for money. She never tried to divvy up my property or ask for my home or business assets—nothing. My divorce attorney dealt with her via email. He would just send her the appropriate documents, she would print and sign them (whether she understood them or not, I don't know), scan them, and email them back to him. I had no further interaction with her, and that was totally fine. So, I was lucky in a way. I don't really cling to material things anyway, and at that point, I was so down, another blow was something I almost expected. I was walking around with this impending sense of doom, waiting for the other shoe to drop so it would be all over.

Today, I feel much better, and I am so glad I made it through. I would love to get married again. I waited fifty-three years for my first marriage, putting it off until a time when I could really focus on it. I had traveled all over the country playing basketball and being so immersed in my career that I really couldn't pay attention to marriage before then. I knew I couldn't do both things well; one would suffer. As a professional basketball player, I did not want my career to suffer. As a small business owner, I did not want my business to suffer, so I waited until my business was mature enough to be run by the management group I had in place.

I would love to get married again. I'm also still very involved with the Chinese community and plan to stay involved because I enjoy Chinese culture, and I have so many wonderful Chinese friends. I would even possibly like to find another Chinese wife. Hopefully, I will find someone I can really click with. I don't think that's difficult, but it's not as easy as you might think. Plus, I learned long ago that even when I put my Plan A, Plan B, and Plan C together, in the end, it's God's plan; whatever God has laid out for me is what the plan will be. So I've learned not to get too attached to any future hopes and just make sure I can do the best I can do.

QUESTIONS FOR REFLECTION

Have you ever had your heart broken? What did you learn from it?

_____

_____

_____

Whether it's love or some goal you had that failed, what did you do to pick yourself up and get back into the game?

_____

_____

_____

Do you think it's true that people make plans but God's plan overrules them? If so, when has that been your experience, and what did you learn from it?

_____

_____

_____

If you are struggling now, what would you ask God to do for you? Write your prayer below:

_____

_____

_____

Chapter 5

MY SUPPORT GROUP

While I was going through my divorce and the darkness and despair that accompanied it, I was reaching out to medical professionals for consultations and prescription medications. The next thing I did was assemble a group of close friends I'd known for thirty or forty years. By design, this group consisted of about five men approximately my age. Two, however, were older: Coach George Raveling, who had coached me at Washington State University from 1975 to 1979, and Coach Lenny Wilkens who had coached me on the Seattle Super-Sonics from 1980 to 1983.

George Raveling and I had stayed in touch through the years and become even closer recently. It was really good to see and talk to him about everything I was going through. He had some keen words of advice for me at this time. "Here I was at sixty years of age," he said, "thinking that life was over and I'd never make anything out of myself again. Then my big opportunity came at sixty-three." (George is eighty-two now.)

For decades, George had been building a reputation as one of the top coaches and had led several championship-caliber teams. He was a very good coach and an excellent mentor and friend, but he had never quite achieved the kind of success he wanted in becoming a championship coach at the NCAA level. Then at age sixty-three, he went to work for Nike. For the last twenty years, he has been working as Nike's global marketing person in mainland China, the world's biggest marketing territory. I've met with George in China a couple of times, and I talk to him frequently. George was very understanding about what I was going through, especially when I explained that none of it was really my doing; life had just taken its turn.

George was gracious enough to help me with a little money toward my mortgage payments for two or three months, which helped out quite a bit. I will never forget his generosity, but more importantly, his words of wisdom stayed with me about how his big break did not come until he was sixty-three. Here I was at only sixty years of age. He reminded me, "James, your best days are ahead of you." I never forget that and I do now think my best years are ahead of me, working with my nonprofit foundation, running for elected office in Seattle, speaking professionally around the country to students and student athletes. There's so much that I still want to get out there and do with my life, which is one of the main reasons I decided not to end my life. I will never forget George Raveling, and I'm so thankful he never forgot me.

Lenny Wilkens, my Seattle SuperSonics coach in the NBA, is an all-star, all-class, all-the-time guy. Here he was, over eighty years of age, yet taking the time to understand what

I was going through and allowing me to meet with him almost monthly throughout 2018, to be there for me. Lenny also came to the hospital a couple of times when I was in intensive care after my 2015 open-heart surgery. He told me a couple of times that he looked directly into my eyes and thought I recognized him and knew he was there; although, I have absolutely no recollection of that. Other folks also told me he came, but I couldn't remember it for the life of me.

During our monthly breakfast meetings in 2018, he helped me figure out what I had to look forward to. He got so excited when I told him I was thinking about starting a nonprofit foundation and possibly running for city council. Those goals right away told people I at least had some hope and something to live for. Hope is the one thing you really lose sight of when you're in the midst of depression. Even something as seemingly trivial as staying alive to take care of your dog so it won't be lonely gives a suicidal person a sense of hope and purpose.

Another instrumental person in my group was a business partner, Brad Meyers. Brad was a former collegiate and all-star high school basketball hotshot, who went to my alma mater, Washington State University. Brad is a really good friend who was right there for me. Since we were also business partners, we had more reason than just my health to check in with each other. He was someone I could text at 2 a.m. to say I didn't think I was going to make it through the night. Thanks to his responsiveness, I did. Brad's been there throughout and still is.

Another great friend was John Stimac. John and I have known each other for about thirty-five years. We have been golf buddies and dear friends. John was constantly at the hospital with me throughout my intensive care stay. He made sure my wife had transportation back and forth to the hospital, and he would take her and her son down to the cafeteria for a bite to eat every now and then. John basically took over a lot of the essential elements of my life when I was out of commission, and he's been so good with everything and such a great friend throughout. He really understood the dire straits I was in, and how close I came to exiting this world, both from the emergency open-heart surgery and via my own hands. He's been there for me through it all.

Another valuable friend during this time was Chuck Wright. Chuck is a mental health professional. He has worked for several years with the Donaldson Clinic to provide mental health therapy to patients and their families who needed that while going through physical therapy. Chuck and I have been close friends for about fifteen years. His perspective as a mental health professional was really helpful in understanding what I was going through. He told me that just by having a small objective, a small goal in front of you, a suicidal person can have a sense of hope—and hope is the best thing we can ask for.

One day, I asked Chuck if "suicide is always an option." I told him that even now, I occasionally have suicidal thoughts flowing through my mind if I'm struggling with something I don't feel I can handle. Those situations are becoming increasingly rare. I probably have them less than once a month.

And then, they are just fleeting thoughts. Chuck told me that, yes, for someone who's been on the verge of suicide, unfortunately, suicide will always be an option.

For someone who hasn't gone through mental anguish like mine, suicide is also an option but way down on the list. If you look at fifty options for coping with a difficult situation, suicide might be number fifty for someone with a healthy mindset who is genuinely happy. For someone who has been suicidal in the past, suicide would probably be in the top five or ten options for dealing with a stressful situation. So, for now, suicide is always there as an option for me. Someday, when I'm totally back to normal and feeling healthy and happy about my life like I used to be, suicidal thoughts might drop down to the fiftieth position where they ought to be.

So that was the group of friends I really turned to throughout my crisis: successful people, business people, people who have gone through life's ups and downs themselves. I reached out to men, and my old coaches in particular, because men tend to put together game plans. Having been an athlete coached by great coaches, I thought maybe all I needed was a game plan, and then I could go out there and execute the play for the coach. That made us a great team. So that's what really helped me start navigating my way out of darkness.

I had many female friends who were there for me as well, but as individuals rather than a collective group. They would call to check in with me on occasion. There's a difference in what men and what women typically offer in these situations.

Men typically put together a game plan to get from point A to point B. Women come in with a lot more empathy, and a lot more ways to try to heal you emotionally from the inside out, starting with your own inner soul. They also would bring me things like herbal teas, scented candles, and chocolates. They'd share poems and Bible verses with me. They would pull up a particular song or two from YouTube and send it to me, or they might bake a tray of cookies for me. All those things were appreciated, and they made me feel good in the moment, but this guy at least, along with all that female nurturing, really needed a game plan to execute. So keep that in mind when you or someone you know is going through a suicidal crisis. Men and women need different things, we desire different things, and we respond differently to different things. All in all, everything actually helps in the long run, but we always want to help someone get through a crisis and back to their old selves again as quickly as possible.

So, having these friends for support is what largely got me through 2018. I asked that group of fellows, "When I wake up at 2 a.m. and can't get back to sleep, can I call you?" They all said, "Yes, right away. Put me on speed dial." I also let them know I needed them to check in on me two or three times a week. Up until then, the only time the phone was ringing was from debt collectors or people trying to serve me legal summons, so the vast majority of my phone calls were doing nothing but adding to my stress. It did wonders for me to pick up the phone knowing a friend was calling who actually cared about me and didn't want anything from me other than to see how my day was going, to hear what kinds of thoughts I was having, and to learn what I was being bothered by at that particular moment.

I encourage all of you out there to put together your own small, intimate group of people you can count on and feel very comfortable with. To feel loved and supported are two of the things a suicidal person needs more than anything. Unfortunately, when you are in that deep, dark, and desperate place, feeling loved and supported is the last thing you feel. So be there for others no matter what.

Questions for Reflection

Who has been there for you when you've been depressed or in a crisis? What did they do to help you feel better?

_____

_____

_____

If you are feeling isolated or depressed right now, make a list of all the people you could reach out to for help or just a listening ear. After making your list, choose one person and reach out to them. Then challenge yourself to reach out to the other people on your list, even if it's just one per day, until you have a solid support group.

Chapter 6

A MOMENT OF REFLECTION

Here I am in 2019, enjoying a beautiful Seattle spring day, with 2018 finally pretty much in my rearview mirror. All I can do is thank God that I did not take my life, and for that, I feel so grateful and tremendously blessed. It is hard now to believe that just a few months earlier, I had even entertained those thoughts.

I just got in from walking my dog around the neighborhood. The Seattle sky is the purest blue you can imagine. Majestic Mount Rainier seems to hover over the horizon, with its still, snowcapped peak. A beautiful sight to behold.

During my walk, I chatted with a few of my neighbors. A handful of them received a handwritten Christmas letter from me letting them know exactly what I'd been through in 2018. They've been wonderful, occasionally checking in on me and saying hello when I walk past their homes.

Moments like these are when you really learn to cherish life's little things. It was so nice to feel the sun shining on my face, to hear the birds chirping, to see the squirrels running here and there gathering their nuts, to watch my dog excitedly greet other dogs as we passed them, and to see neighborhood kids on the playing field starting up their spring baseball or soccer games. I realize now how much I would have missed all of those little things if I were not still alive.

I was inspired to name my foundation Your Gift of Life after a song of the same name by Teddy Pendergrass. In the song's lyrics, he says how much he likes the sunshine, likes cloudy days, likes the rain, likes the snow, and likes to hear the wind blow. Those words are so poignant for me because that's exactly how I now feel. It's amazing to think within the last year, I was in such a dark place that I felt nobody loved me and nobody would miss me.

I have plenty of things to look forward to now, including the opportunity to raise mental health awareness and help prevent suicides. Through this book, I hope, if you or someone you know is going through this deep, dark valley with seemingly no way out, I can provide some tools to help. I can say, firsthand, that it's well worth hanging in there to see the daylight again.

Ending my life would have been, without a doubt, the stupidest decision I ever made. All I can say, over and over again, is, "I'm so glad I'm here to enjoy all these wonderful blessings."

I'm still striving to put my life back together. Working on behalf of my foundation has become one of my main focuses. I've also decided to run for Seattle City Council. I'm also coping with some loneliness. While a lot of great friends have helped me through my dark times, no one has been intimate with me, lying beside me to give me physical and emotional comfort. I miss all of that, and I am looking to restore that part of my life. I would love to get married again, this time to someone who genuinely loves me as I will genuinely love her, so we can make our life together for the rest of our journey. But I've learned there are a lot of things we cannot control, and personal relationship choices, even ones that change our lives drastically, are among the things we cannot control. However, we have to trust and believe the best about people; otherwise, we go around feeling paranoid, skeptical, and jaded, which keeps us from enjoying life and living it to the fullest. I can't wait to get back to living my life that way again.

My health is better, but I will never again be what I was physically. Until I was about fifty-six, I was jogging three or four days a week, three to four miles at a time. I did it with ease, with my running partner, rain or shine. Now, I get winded just walking a couple of blocks down the street with my dog. I have to accept the reality that my body has gone through some tremendous stress and damage.

Still, what a blessing it is to be alive. When my cardiologist was asked, he said, "James should have died that day." Those words continue to remind me how close I came to losing my life. Even during those early days after surgery, I felt myself hovering between life and death in an otherworldly way I will never forget.

My words of encouragement to everyone reading this book are, no matter how hard things get, keep hanging in there. I guarantee, at some point the darkness will lift and there will be daylight ahead. Your sense of hope will be restored and you, too, will realize how tremendously blessed you are.

Please continue to reach out to each other for support, encouragement, and a shoulder to lean on. We need to do that for each other. I particularly want men to learn to open up and talk about more than last night's game. We can do it. I've learned to do it, and I feel really comfortable doing it with everybody now. Just sitting down with people, sharing my story, and more importantly, listening to their stories can make all the difference in someone's life.

QUESTIONS FOR REFLECTION

Take a moment to do a mental health check. What are you struggling with right now?

_____

_____

_____

List three people you trust that you can talk to about your feelings:

1. _____

2. _____

3. _____

List three suicide prevention assets (help line, etc.) that you have access to:

1. _____

2. _____

3. _____

Write an outline of your "getting back on my feet" game plan:

What can you do today to make yourself feel better? It can be as simple as going for a walk or playing a favorite song. Make a list of ways you can try to cheer yourself up:

_____

_____

_____

_____

_____

_____

_____

_____

_____

_____

Chapter 7

IF I'D GONE THROUGH WITH IT

I know it's kind of gruesome to think about, but one thing most people want to know if someone does take their own life is how they did it. Usually the "how" is part of the stigma and cover-up we don't talk about.

There are lots of ways to end one's life. I'm not going to go into all of them and give anyone any ideas they haven't already thought of, but I will discuss the three methods I considered.

Before I do, let me clarify that all my life I've really prided myself on living a healthy lifestyle and being in good health. I never in any way abuse my body. I have never, ever smoked a cigarette, smoked a joint, drank a drop of alcohol, or done any illegal drugs. That has been my choice.

When I was ten, I remember returning home from school one day when one of my favorite uncles was visiting us. There he was, sprawled out on our living room sofa, reeking from alcohol and totally incoherent. I promised myself then, "That will never happen to me." It's been a choice for me ever since not to abuse my body. I even went to the number-one drinking and partying school in the late '70s, Washington State University, and abstained. All of my friends could not wait to drink; some of them would even begin on Thursday afternoon, getting sloshed for the weekend. The drinking age was twenty-one in Washington, but just eight miles away over the border was Moscow, Idaho, where the drinking age was eighteen. A caravan of cars full of WSU students would head over there every weekend to have a good time. My friends would beg and plead with me to go with them, but I never did. I had promised myself at age ten never to lose control of myself due to drugs or alcohol. I've kept that promise all these years, and I plan to continue keeping it for the rest of my life.

In China, it's the custom to drink alcohol with meals, especially during business lunches when deals are being made. The rice wine flows freely, and everyone around the table will drink shots left and right, and finally, after dinner, stagger home. I've never engaged in that. I told all my Chinese friends when I first started going to China that I didn't drink, smoke, or do drugs. (And I'm vegetarian on top of that!) They thought I was some type of Buddhist monk, but I told them it is just my personal preference for how I live my life. After trying to pressure me a little, they have all learned to respect my choice, and even though I feel like the odd man out every time the rice wine starts flowing, I'm able to hang on to my dignity and sense of myself.

My vegetarian diet (which I've observed for more than thirty-five years) also throws off my Chinese friends. The newly affluent Chinese do not hesitate in rolling out mounds of different types of meat for every meal. It's another custom I just

86

don't partake in, so they always manage to have a little vegetarian fare for me.

You've got to have some convictions that you'll stick to no
matter what. And that's how I've lived my life. I make this
point about my health and convictions because, in terms of
ways I considered committing suicide, I had no alcohol or
drugs of any kind in my house to overdose on. I am also not a
gun owner. I had to rule out these typical methods of suicide
unless I chose to go through the extra effort of developing a
serious and sudden drug or alcohol problem and buying a gun.
Just having to make that transition from my normal life gave
me pause enough to stop me from acting impulsively and doing something I would later regret.

However, in my garage's rafters, I had coiled up a rope about
thirty-feet long and three-quarters of an inch thick. It had been
up there for twenty years at least. Every day when I drove into
my garage, I'd glance up to see the rope coiled there, and note
all the places I could easily loop the rope over before tying it
around my neck and kicking the chair out from underneath
me. That was my preferred method if I was going to do harm
to myself.

The second method was also hanging from the same rafters. It
was several feet of rubber tubing, about four inches in diame-
ter, which was used as a sump pump that I periodically drained
my hot tub with. It, too, had sat up there for several years. My
thought was to attach one end of the hose to my exhaust pipe,
crack the car window, and put the other end in it. All of the

other windows would be closed, and I would close the garage door behind me, start the car, and sit in it, waiting for carbon monoxide to take my life. I don't know anything about that method, other than the things I've heard or seen very briefly, so I had no idea how long it might take. Would I be suffering in agony, or peacefully fall asleep? I didn't know, and I wasn't in any hurry to find out.

The third and final way I was thinking about ending my life was "suicide by cop." Being a very large and tall African-American man makes it much more difficult for me to get out of a situation involving law enforcement alive. Even though I have a lot of personal friends in the Seattle Police Department, my thought was to go up to a police officer and wrestle him for his gun. I was certain either he or one of his partners would shoot me dead on the spot. Not "shoot to wound" but "shoot to kill" as we have seen in so many examples around this country during our lifetimes. If I were white, I might be given the benefit of the doubt. But as an African-American man, I have witnessed and experienced the racist attitudes and prejudice that persists in this country that every person of color puts up with each and every day. I knew messing with a cop's gun was a sure way out of this life if I chose it.

I hate to think that because, as I mentioned, I have several friends who are Seattle police officers. They are wonderful people. But I've always wondered why, when an African-American man is shot by a police officer in this country, he isn't just wounded in his leg, arm, or shoulder. Instead, he is usually shot multiple times to ensure he is dead. That has always bothered me, and it still does. I am just happy that I didn't have to find out for myself to prove my point.

So those were the three ways I seriously contemplated ending my life. The first two methods often left me with a pit in the bottom of my stomach when I thought about how long it might take for someone to discover my body. I live in a house set off from the street a good fifty feet or so, as are all the other houses in the neighborhood. Plus, I have frosted, plate glass windows near the front door, and once I close my garage door, you can't really tell I'm home. There might be a light on or two, but that's really no big indication of whether I'm home or not. I've always had lights set to timers that come on and off. It was also normal for me to stay in the house for two or three days in a row, since I didn't feel like going to the gym every day anymore.

I mentioned these three ways of ending my life to both my family doctor and my mental health professional friend, Chuck Wright. The first thing my doctor told me was to make sure I got rid of that coil of rope in my rafters. And he couldn't stress enough that I should not dillydally but go straight home after my appointment and remove the rope and give it to one of my neighbors or friends. I did just that; I took it down and put it in a large, plastic garbage bag. Then I gave it to Chuck. Chuck still has that rope to this day.

Chuck told me that my concern over how people would discover my body gave me a sense of hope in itself that I was seriously lacking at the time. He breathed a sigh of relief when I told him that was my concern.

One thing we need to look for in anybody with suicidal ideations is that faint glimmer of hope that just might still be there. It might be a simple thing like wondering: Who's going to take care of my pet? Who's going to take in the mail? Who's going to water the plants? When someone is dealing with suicidal ideations, they're not thinking too far beyond themselves, but they do care about those things close to them, such as pets and favorite plants.

I'm so glad I made it past that point. I was overcome at that time by impulsiveness. I've never been impulsive in my life. I've always been very thoughtful, methodical, and purposeful as I think things through. But when that impulsiveness became part of my mindset, I would hear a little voice in my head telling me, "Go ahead and do it. Do it now. You've already planned it out. Just go ahead and do it." That was scary. It was difficult not only to get that voice to quiet down and go away, but to actually resist the urge to act before I could think. That was probably the scariest time when I was working my way out of the depths.

I encourage you, no matter what your preferred means of ending your life may be, to think twice, think thrice, and keep thinking. Don't give in to the impulsive nature that often comes over us when we are in that place. If you have a gun around the house, get rid of it! If you have alcohol around the house, get rid of it! If you have drugs around the house, get rid of them! If you have a coil of rope hanging up in your rafters, get rid of it! If nothing else, you can have a close friend or neighbor hang onto those possessions until you've worked your way back to a healthy state of mind.

For me, all I do is think about how glad I am I didn't end up killing myself.

QUESTIONS FOR REFLECTION

What glimmers of hope can you hold onto—things you care or worry about being taken care of if you were gone?

_____

_____

_____

What accessible items must you remove so you are not tempted?

_____

_____

_____

Stop reading now and get rid of those items. After you do so, write down how you feel now that you have removed them.

Chapter 8

GOD IS SO REAL TO ME

I don't want to get overly preachy in this book, but I will say that whatever your convictions, spiritual beliefs, or religious tendencies (I'm a lifelong Christian Baptist), there comes a point in everyone's life when we become convinced there has to be a Higher Power out there somewhere.

When I was in the depths of my despair, feeling alone and absolutely without any hope for a tomorrow, I knew one thing for sure: God was right there with me. God was there when I would cry out in the middle of the night and couldn't get back to sleep. God was there to give me enough strength for one more day. God loved me, even when I didn't love myself and helped me find a purpose. I just knew God was there with me, holding my hand and steadying me. If I had been holding God's hand, I surely would have let go a long time ago. Instead, God was holding mine.

When I went through my emergency open-heart surgery in 2015, God brought me through with a renewed sense of compassion and a love for all humanity. When I went through my mental challenges in 2017–2018, God brought me through with a renewed sense of empathy for everyone, no matter their station. I will never again minimalize what someone else might be going through. I get it now!

I came out of this mental health challenge with a sense of why I was still here: to help others undergoing mental health challenges and to help with suicide prevention. After what I've been through, I have a story to tell, and I also want to share my strategy—how I made it through and how you can make it through as well.

QUESTIONS FOR REFLECTION

What evidence have you experienced of a Higher Power?

_____

_____

_____

_____

_____

_____

Take time now to pray to God or whatever you choose to call your Higher Power to help you through your difficulties. If you are not used to praying, you can say the prayer below to help you get started.

Dear God,

I am at the end of my rope. I need help. I am without hope. You are my last hope. Please help me to feel hope again. Help me to know you are with me through this, and even if it doesn't get better today or tomorrow, it will get better eventually, and you will be with me until the end. Help me to believe that a brighter day lies ahead. Help me to become excited about that amazing day in my future when you will reveal this situation has all been part of your plan for me to help me become stronger and better able to serve others. Amen.

Commit to saying this prayer, or your own prayer every morning, evening, and as often as you need to.

Lenny Wilkens and James at Breakfast

George Raveling and James at A Plus Event

James, Stan, Kathy and Kym & Ryan Hilinski

James doing a Basketball Camp in China

James Donaldson on Mental Health

James at NAMI Conference in Seattle, 2019.
He became a member of the Board of Directors with the Seattle Chapter in 2020.

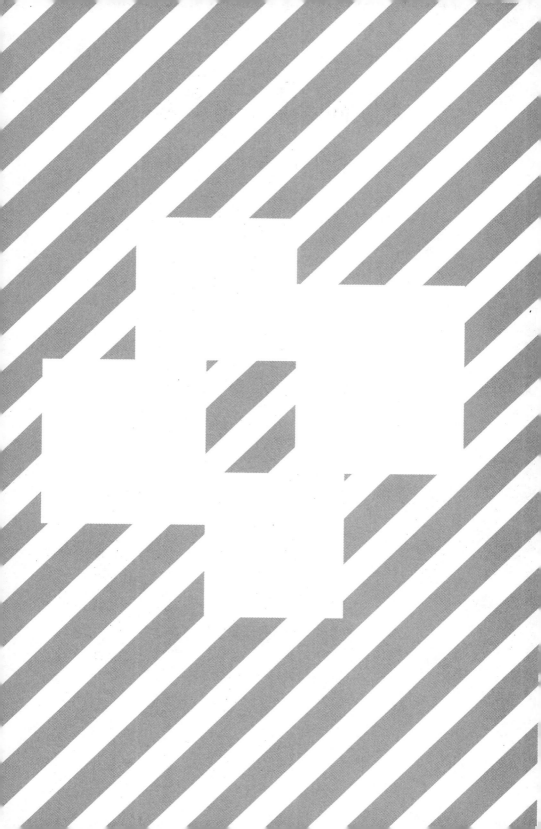

Chapter 9

FIND A REASON TO KEEP LIVING

During my basketball career, I had to go up against the great Michael Jordan of the Chicago Bulls when he was in his prime. I consider him one of the greatest basketball players of all time. Michael has related that during his childhood, he wasn't that good at basketball. Sometimes he would be left off the team because he wasn't good enough. When he was cut from his junior high basketball team, he set his mind to showing all those who doubted him that he was indeed good enough to play. That was the beginning of his great basketball career.

During Michael's professional career, the doubters came out of the woodwork again, questioning whether he would ever become a team player instead of a great all-around individual player. He took that criticism as motivation as well. Even though he remained one of the best individual NBA players at the time, before long, he became the team leader and was helping his teammates succeed, resulting in the team becoming championship contenders.

But that wasn't enough. The doubters came out again, wondering if Michael Jordan and the Bulls could defeat first the Boston Celtics, and then the Detroit "Bad Boys," the Pistons.

Those two teams had been the Bulls' nemesis for three or four years before Jordan could finally get past them to start the Bulls' championships run.

Michael used the doubters and rivals to motivate himself, becoming one of the best NBA players of all time, not just as an individual, but as a six-time NBA World Champion and six-time World Championship Finals MVP. Michael found that he could turn a negative—all those folks who doubted him—into a positive, showing everyone around him they were wrong. He showed it through his exemplary play on the court, not by running his mouth.

When I was down and out in my darkest days of depression, anxiety, and suicidal ideations, I similarly had a couple of moments I used as a catalyst to keep moving forward. One was the unfortunate situation of Tyler Hilinski, an up-and-coming Washington State University star quarterback who was slated to become the starting quarterback the following year. In January 2018, Tyler took his own life by shooting himself on campus.

Immediately, the newspapers and social media sites were flooded with people who knew Tyler trying to tell the story of his life and how wonderful he was. That shook me to my inner core. I told myself, "I just don't want anybody out there telling the story of my life. I want to tell my story." That was one of my main motivations to get out of my deepest, darkest place.

I don't know why Tyler's situation became such a catalyst for me. Maybe it was because he was a student athlete walking the very same campus I had forty years before. When the reports mentioned some of the buildings and apartment complexes on campus, I knew exactly where they were. I have been back to that campus many times and still have a close affiliation with WSU, so I think in that regard I closely identified with Tyler. It was a very unfortunate incident, but I was able to use it to finally get myself up and moving toward finding my way out.

Another catalyst, which I previously mentioned, happened in July 2018, when I was in the hospital for complications following surgery and the National Basketball Retired Players Association decided to kick me off its board. Having the board kick me when I was down actually made me want to fight for my dignity. I wasn't going to commit suicide and let any of the people who had mistreated me use it as further "proof" I had been unfit to remain on the board.

My point is, you need to find a reason and purpose to hang in there and keep going. It can be anything really—whatever is important to you. Some people have pets they want to continue taking care of. That's a reason and a purpose. Other people have children or parents who depend on them. That's a reason and a purpose. Other people have their life's work yet to complete, and they want to stick around to finish it. Whatever it is, find it, grab onto it, and make it your reason and purpose to keep on living.

You'll be so glad you did; in fact, you'll find that once you get through those depressing, anxiety-filled days, the rainbow on the other side of the darkness is well worth it.

I encourage you as much as I possibly can to find something that matters to you and make it your catalyst for coming out of the darkness.

QUESTIONS FOR REFLECTION

Think of a difficult time in the past. What catalysts got you through it?

_____

_____

_____

Now think of your current difficult situation. What catalysts might keep you going?

_____

_____

_____

If you are not considering suicide but know someone else who may be, what catalysts might you suggest for them? Make your list and then share it with them.

Chapter 10

WORKING YOUR WAY BACK TO YOUR OLD SELF

Please keep in mind that working your way back to your old self requires time, patience, and an understanding that it won't happen overnight. One thing you have to keep in mind in getting back to normal is that you're still in a somewhat fragile state. Some days you'll feel wonderful, but other days you'll be down in the dumps. This rollercoaster ride is totally normal. You've gone through a lot, and you haven't yet found that equilibrium you had before everything turned upside down. I know we live in a fast-paced world where people want instant gratification; however, this is one of the few times when you must realize that getting back to your old self takes time and a lot of self-care, and that can take some time.

There's no rush. If you need more time away from work, request it. If you need your friends to check in on you more often, ask them to do so. If you need to have a good cry, by all means, cry until you can't cry anymore. It's good to get it out of your system, and it's healthy for you.

This advice especially goes for men; we men grew up being told boys don't cry. We carry that into manhood, only to find it locks us into a virtual cage from which there seems to be no escape. We aren't used to crying, and we definitely do not want to cry in front of anyone else, but when we put our heads down on the pillow, hoping for a good night's sleep, and our emotions come over us, as they sometimes will, we have to allow ourselves to cry.

Allow yourself to blubber away like a little baby. Allow yourself to fall asleep on a tear-soaked pillow. You will realize how much better you feel after you get it out of your system.

I was crying all the time when I was working my way back to my old self. I cried myself to sleep many times. Other times, I would pick up the phone and call someone I knew cared about me and cry to them about everything I was going through. I'd also be a listening ear for other folks who were going through similar things, and we would cry together. I'd cry every time I listened to Teddy Pendergrass' song "This Gift of Life." It reminds me of how close I came to throwing away this wonderful gift of life. I've found that crying is good for you. It helps to release the pain, and you always feel better after.

As I mentioned, there really is no rush to get back to normal, whatever normal is for you. It's all a process, and you'll soon find those folks who have been with you through the most crucial of times will gradually ease up and get back to their own lives and concerns. It's easy for them to forget about you if you don't remind them that you still need them.

This happened to me several times during my recovery. One guy in my intimate circle of friends does a lot of talking but very little follow-through. To give him credit, he really cared about me and was a good friend; he did tend to check in on me more often than the others in my group in the beginning. But then, as he saw me starting to stabilize somewhat, he let up on calling and checking in on me. When I tried to contact him, he was very slow to respond. That's a prime example of someone who is there for you at first, but then gets back to their own busy life and tends to forget about you. I had to remind him over and over that he was one of my go-to guys, and when I call, I'm calling because I *need* to talk to him. He tried to be more responsive, but actually got worse as time went on. He kept making coffee or lunch dates with me, only to reschedule time and time again. After being stood up a few times, I finally told him I was tired of holding my breath to see if he would come through for me. He could see then I was serious and still in a very fragile state. Things didn't get much better between us after that, but I'm glad to say they didn't get much worse.

Similarly, I realized I couldn't rush back into dating because of my depression. I started trying to date again with several women I met at Match.com. I'd used this dating site before when I was on top of my game and had no problem meeting a number of great women, several of whom are still my friends. But this time, it seemed like I had a sign on my forehead that said "loser," and they could see it from a mile away. Time after time, I would message someone on the dating site; we would seem to hit it off pretty well, so we would meet at a restaurant. I'd drive halfway across town to meet her and spend at least $100 on dinner for the two of us, which I couldn't afford at the time. Things would seem to go very well over dinner. Even though I am a nondrinker, I never minded being the gentleman and buying her a drink if that's what she wanted, even though it's usually what ran up the bill.

These dates would go well, and I would be filled with all kinds of anticipation and excitement for a follow-up a few days later, only to have her suddenly disappear. She wouldn't return messages or phone calls, sometimes even hiding her profile from me, even though we had ended the evening saying how wonderful it was to meet each other. I've since learned that this behavior is called "ghosting." This must have happened ten or fifteen times during my recovery. I kept thinking, *Damn, how many more body blows can a guy take?* I could not figure out what I had done wrong to turn them off, but maybe my depression or neediness was seeping through, which made it clear I wasn't yet ready for a serious relationship and needed to work more on myself first.

So, I had to learn to just slow everything down, keep my expectations low, and try not to do more than was reasonable in my situation. Every day I took it one step at a time for several months. It was a long, slow process, but I finally made it through.

Being a lifelong athlete, I knew all the benefits of physical exercise, and the feel-good endorphins they create within your brain, but because I was still recovering from open-heart surgery, and probably from being depressed, I just didn't feel like exercising, so I didn't do nearly enough to help myself.

I did finally get back into it after a few months, mainly to be around a lot of positive people in an uplifting, clean, sunlit gym. Now I'm back to exercising at least five days a week like I have done for the last forty years. And I feel wonderful.

QUESTIONS FOR REFLECTION

Are you holding back tears? Commit to releasing them. Schedule a time to focus on your feelings and let the tears flow. Write down that time now and keep your appointment.

How did crying make you feel?

_____

_____

_____

Do you enjoy exercise? Which physical activities can you participate in to release endorphins and begin to feel better?

_____

_____

_____

Chapter 11

GET BACK IN TOUCH WITH YOURSELF AND THOSE AROUND YOU

One thing that really exacerbates the loneliness and isolation of depression and anxiety is the conflicting feelings of needing people and not wanting to be around them. When you're depressed, you naturally don't feel like hanging out with people or letting them see you are down. You tend to spend time alone, avoiding friends and associates. However, with isolation, unhappy thoughts start compounding.

This tendency to isolate ourselves is one of the best reasons to form an intimate little group of people who will be there for you throughout your struggles. These can all be people you meet with individually, such as a best friend, pastor or priest, or mentor, etc. You just need to have more than one person for support so you don't dump everything on one person and exhaust them, and also so you get multiple perspectives and ideas for how to get through your struggles.

It's also good to start remembering the little things that make life so special. Take time to stop and smell the roses, and remember that's what life is all about.

In our current technological age, it's so easy to disconnect from real and personal relationships and just feel like everything is okay because you get a lot of likes on Facebook. When it comes down to it, none of that social media stuff adds up to much in the real world.

When I was going through my dark time and the holidays rolled around, I took the time for the first time in several years to personally write and mail Christmas cards to quite a few of my friends around the country. Years ago, I used to do that kind of thing regularly. As a matter of fact, I used to be quite the letter writer. Dating back to my early twenties, I wrote hundreds, if not thousands, of handwritten postcards and letters to so many dear friends. But, like most of us, I got away from all of that. Once I got back into handwriting letters and actually feeling the pen, paper, and envelope, and putting the stamp on, and dropping it in the mail, I started to feel closer to people than I had in years.

That's one the things I recommend—getting out of the fast-paced hustle and bustle world you live in and just slowing down and getting back to the basics.

Another thing I did was personally hand-deliver about a dozen Christmas cards to my neighbors with a Christmas letter inside. Even though we were neighbors, most of them really didn't know what I was going through. In the letter, I told them what I'd been through that year, and that, even though I was starting to feel a little better, I would appreciate it if they would check in on me from time to time.

And guess what? Several of them did check in on me right away, and they continue to do so.

I've had some heart-to-heart conversations with neighbors who experienced some very difficult times of their own and didn't have anyone to turn to. They applauded the fact that I let them know what I was going through.

Making contact though postcards, cards, and letters helps you feel connected. I know it's hard to put our cell phones down and spend time with another person, looking them in the eye, maybe grasping their hands, and even letting a tear roll down your cheek, but that is realness to the nth degree.

Over the last year or two, I feel like I've made deep and genuine friendships I'm sure will last the rest of my life. Plus, those I've reconnected with feel like they have reconnected with me as well. I recommend making these small gestures that bring joy to life.

I travel to China quite a bit. The last couple of times, I went to Goodwill or Value Village first to pick up a couple of dozen children's books (that still looked virtually brand-new) and then hand them out to young kids in China. They're trying to learn English, and these simple little books help them to do so.

But more than anything, since China is such a gift-giving society, it really goes a long way toward creating lasting friendships. Most importantly, it makes me feel good to put a smile on a little child's face. I can't help but smile and feel great about it myself.

Put your creative hat on and think of various acts of kindness that could put a smile on people's faces and make you feel good inside. It truly works.

QUESTIONS FOR REFLECTION

Which relationship-enhancing activities that you once enjoyed, such as letter writing or playing cards with friends, have you stopped participating in? How can you resurrect those activities?

_____

_____

_____

_____

Have you ever reached out to someone and been surprised by the positive results? How did it make you feel?

_____

_____

_____

_____

What small acts of kindness can you begin doing to put a smile on people's faces?

_____

_____

_____

Do one of those small acts of kindness now, and then come back and write about how it made you feel.

Chapter 12

KEEPING AGREEMENTS WITH YOURSELF

While I truly believe most people have good intentions, life is so busy these days that it's hard to focus on anything except yourself and your own needs. That doesn't mean most people are self-centered. They are just trying to survive from day to day. Consequently, they will be oblivious to others' needs unless you bring those needs to their direct attention.

Today may be the most stressful time in human history, especially with twenty-four-hour business, news, and constant distractions, plus the coronavirus pandemic affecting us all. Family life has become very chaotic, and we have workplaces we don't enjoy going to. People have little time to think of anything other than trying to get through their own crazy day.

As I told you in Chapter 3, I was kicked pretty hard when I was down—in a hospital bed fighting to recover from open-heart surgery—but I used it as motivation to pick myself up, dust myself off, and keep working toward getting back to my old self. My athletic training had taught me to persevere no matter the odds. Even when you're down by twenty points in the fourth quarter, you can't give up because you never know when the tide will turn, and you'll have to be ready to take advantage of the opportunity.

I've always been very easy-going. I'm not easily rattled, but a methodical, thoughtful, and step-by-step kind of guy. I'm still pretty much that way, but after what I'd been through, I decided I would be in charge of my life from then on. Coming so close to the brink of suicide, I place so much more value on my life than I ever did before. I'm still a really nice guy, but there's a bit of an edge to me now that I don't think I acknowledged before. I call it a protective edge because it works like a buffer to protect me from some of life's bumps and bruises. I felt almost like I had to be a little bit of an asshole for the first time in my life, but as long as I remained true to myself, that was okay, and anyone who knew what I'd gone through and supported me would totally understand. If they didn't, they weren't really meant to be around me anyway. Then I would distance myself from them because they were not going to be there when I needed them.

I feel like I know what's best for me. I know how far to push myself. I know that when I get tired, I need to take a break and slow it down to ensure I get my rest. I know not to stress myself out to the point that I become emotionally distraught. I've learned all these things about myself by going through my own mental challenges. That said, I don't know if I'm as coachable as I used to be. To be coachable requires putting your faith and trust in someone, following directions, not asking too many questions, and working toward your goal. I'm a little different now because I feel I finally know what's best for me.

I say all that to tell you to take the opportunity, while working your way back to you, to learn about yourself and to learn what this life actually means to you. Care about yourself more than you ever cared before. Become selfish but in a healthy way by looking after yourself. You can still be a super-nice person, but give yourself permission to be an "asshole" once in a while to protect yourself. When it comes down to it, no one's going to look after you better than you can. Even if you have a spouse right next to you, they won't fully understand everything you're going through because we are all individuals, and each of our experiences is so different. Sure, someone else may have sympathy for you; if they've had a similar experience, they may even have empathy for you, but there's only one you, and you know yourself best.

One of the best books I ever read about taking care of oneself is Don Miguel Ruiz's *The Four Agreements*. I read it about twenty-five years ago, but to this day, I keep the four agreements it recommends you make with yourself as best I can to maintain a balanced and healthy life. The four agreements have prevented me from getting stretched too thin by trying to take care of everyone else instead of myself. It's also taught me not to concern myself too much with what other people think because I have to take care of me.

The four agreements are:

- Be impeccable with your word.
- Don't take anything personally.
- Don't make assumptions.

- Always do your best.

I know—they sound so easy and so simple. But they are actually very difficult to follow each and every day. They are difficult because, as Ruiz tells us, we come into this world as helpless infants, totally dependent on our parents or other grownups for survival. Our parents give us our names, choose what neighborhoods we live in, choose the friends we associate with, choose which schools we will go to, choose which religion we will practice, and influence us with their values. We spend all those developmental years constantly trying to please our parents, often to the point of no longer being who we are but who our parents want us to be.

That's okay when we are very young, but around age eight, we start questioning, "Who am I? Why do I believe what I believe? What makes this world go 'round?" We then develop our innate sense of curiosity looking for the answers.

The first agreement (Be impeccable with your word) is difficult for many people unless they really know their true self because they find themselves living a life that is not truly who they are. It starts with you. If you look in the mirror every morning, and you start off your day by lying to yourself, you'll be lying to everyone you come across throughout the day, trying to keep up the lie you told yourself. That's where it all starts. With mental health issues like depression and anxiety, if you try to fool yourself into believing your mental state is fine, then you are just lying to yourself and not accepting reality. This is why it's very important to know one's true self.

After five or six sleepless nights, I knew I wasn't being my true self. Not sleeping is not part of my normal behavior, so I became concerned and called my doctor. I was hoping he could prescribe a simple sleeping pill, but once we started talking about some of the stress I was under, he immediately diagnosed me with depression, anxiety, and suicidal ideations. I don't know if I ever would have come up with that diagnosis on my own, so that's why, when you realize you're not acting like your normal self, it's important to get a medical evaluation as soon as you possibly can. It all boils down to knowing yourself.

The second agreement (Don't take anything personally) is very hard to do. Because, after all, we are people. We care what other people think, especially those we respect, like, and want to be around. We respect our parents from an early age; we would do just about anything to please them. We want to be included, not excluded, from social activities because we are very social beings. We develop this thing called faith, but we're not quite sure what it's all about. We go to school for an education, but it quickly becomes about trying to achieve good grades and competing against our classmates for adoration and recognition. We try out for teams or squads because it's the thing to do. And if we don't do any of these things, we feel tremendous peer pressure/parental pressure. We are made to feel we don't belong, or that we are different and rebellious. Those are very difficult and influential pressures to put upon a young person, so we have to learn not to take any of this personally. Nine times out of ten, when someone is upset with you it's because you didn't fulfill what they wanted you to fulfill. If you look at their own personal baggage, you'll see they are often dumping their own issues on you. Don't take it personally. Be you, and be the best you can be.

The third agreement (Don't make assumptions) is another very difficult agreement to live up to. Our minds work in a way that we naturally make assumptions. And then as we get older, we feel we have enough life experience to just fill in the blanks without all the information, which is jumping to conclusions. It actually becomes easier to make assumptions than to ask or re-ask a question to get a specific answer. If you have difficulty communicating with someone in particular, it's easier just to assume what they might want to communicate to you. However, assumptions, more often than not, will lead you down the wrong path. You have to be careful with making assumptions, even though it's human nature to do so. If you want an answer to your question, ask the question directly. It's not that hard to do, but it is something you have to discipline yourself to do as often as you possibly can.

The last agreement (Always do your best) makes me think about childhood and the childlike innocence that comes with it. Children don't always understand the reasons parents tell them to do certain things, but for the most part, they wish to please their parents. If you tell them to get good grades in school, they will try their darnedest to do so. If you tell them to be quiet and sit still in church, even though they are naturally wiggly, they will try their best to please you.

But as we get older, we learn to cut corners, to take shortcuts to get to our objectives. We learn to lie, cheat, and sometimes do whatever it takes, thinking we are being more efficient and perhaps smarter, but in reality, we're not doing our best to be the best we can be. And only we know within ourselves if we are giving our best effort. As an athlete, I know coaches demand an extremely high level of athletic performance. But you learn, as you go through practice after practice, how to take little shortcuts here and there, how not to totally exert yourself during a particular practice or a drill if you don't have to. But it's funny, especially in sports, how almost every athlete comes alive and becomes much more energetic when they have a chance to score, especially if it will win the game. They can be dead tired on defense, but once a ball bounces to them, they're off to the races. That's a prime example of not always doing your best but saving yourself for situations. Instead, you need to learn to always do your best all the time.

Please keep these four agreements in mind. I know they're impossible to keep every moment of the day, but if you use them as your guiding principles, your life will be much more balanced, healthy, and enjoyable in the long run. Plus, if you don't live your life being the best you can be, it's hard to help anyone else become their best.

> "I cannot be the best me I ought to be, if you are not the best you think you ought to be…. And you cannot be the best you, you ought to be, if I am not the best me that I ought to be."
>
> — Martin Luther King, Jr.

QUESTIONS FOR REFLECTION

Write down a list of all your qualities, tendencies, gifts, preferences, etc. It's important to know yourself. Spend some time writing this list—several days if need be. You may want to use a separate sheet of paper or several sheets of paper for this exercise.

_____

_____

_____

_____

_____

_____

_____

_____

_____

_____

_____

_____

_____

After you make your list, consider how the four agreements relate to you. Write down your thoughts about each one. For example, with the first one, "Be impeccable with your word," write down times when you weren't impeccable with your word and what the results were. Then think of situations where you were and how it benefited you. Next, think of current or upcoming situations where you should be impeccable with your word. Please spend considerable time on this exercise.

Be impeccable with your word.

_____

_____

_____

_____

_____

_____

_____

_____

_____

_____

Don't take anything personally.

_____

_____

_____

_____

_____

_____

_____

_____

Don't make assumptions.

_____

_____

_____

_____

_____

_____

_____

_____

_____

Always do your best.

_____

_____

_____

_____

_____

_____

_____

_____

_____

Chapter 13

WHERE DO I GO FROM HERE?

By the end of 2019, I was feeling better, like I was back on top of things.

I was busy with my nonprofit foundation, Your Gift of Life, and had begun writing this book. I was also doing quite a few speaking engagements, especially to my target audience of young students throughout the United States. When I speak, I make a point of telling the males in the group it's okay to have feelings and that being able to talk about them shows strength to get them to open up and reach out for help if they need it.

Life, however, hasn't been without its trials and tribulations. I hadn't forgotten how my mental health therapist friend Chuck Wright told me that suicide would always be an option for me. Some days I find myself in a funk where I think if just one more shoe drops, I will choose suicide. When I realize I'm in this place, I try to turn that thinking around quickly and break up my routine. I try to find the company of uplifting, positive people whom I know really care about me. I try to change my activities, and maybe go to a coffee shop where quite a few people are around and a lot of conversations are happening, or go to the gym, which is usually an uplifting place as well.

But having that one more shoe drop would be difficult. Let me assess my life now as I'm writing this book so you understand how my mindset has changed from when I felt my life had purpose and I was super-successful.

- ☐ My health is still iffy and probably always will be.
- ☐ I don't have a wife.
- ☐ I don't have any children.
- ☐ My mother passed away.
- ☐ I've never been close to my immediate family, and now we are more estranged than ever.
- ☐ A lot of my friends are no longer around; I am sure they are busy with their lives.
- ☐ I don't have the brick-and-mortar business I had for almost thirty years.
- ☐ I've spent all my NBA savings so I don't have a nest egg for retirement.
- ☐ My home is in foreclosure, and I am barely hanging on to it. (I would end up losing it in July 2020.)

But, when I look around, I also see how truly blessed I am and realize:

- ☐ I'm still a really good guy, of good character, and a good friend to my friends.
- ☐ I still have a wonderful church home that I've been part of for nearly forty years.
- ☐ Most people are still genuinely happy to see and be around me.
- ☐ I've helped countless people through the work I'm doing

with mental health awareness and suicide prevention
- ☐ I realize there is a tomorrow.
- ☐ I realize just how much of a gift life is.

I feel like my life is very much back on track. I've regained a sense of purpose I had totally lost or felt I had totally lost. As you can see from the list above, I have a lot of stressors. Typically, a person can only handle one or two of those things at a time, so when your cup runneth over, like mine did, it really becomes too much to bear.

I'm so glad I'm alive to enjoy life. I can't say it any more plainly than that.

Sure, some days I'm tired physically, mentally, and emotionally, but when those days hit me, I remind myself just to take a step back, remember what I've gone through, and realize no matter what lies ahead, it's not the end of the world until it actually is the end of the world.

When I was going through my very impulsive stage, simple little things like having my cellphone service cut off were enough to send me over the edge. Now I look back at it and realize even though I had to go three days without a cellphone, that was really trivial and not the insurmountable problem it seemed like at the time.

Now, I'm working on saving my home from foreclosure. I worked with my mortgage company throughout 2019. They suggested we try to do a loan modification, but because I'm unemployed, have health issues, have huge medical bills, and my monthly NBA pension is barely enough to pay my mortgage, we're kind of at an impasse. I reached out to some friends who would like to buy the home out of foreclosure, if the mortgage company allows that, and then possibly rent it back to me so I can at least stay here for the time being. I'm hoping that will happen, but for now, my home is in pre-foreclosure and in front of a foreclosure attorney for review.

I was engaged throughout much of 2019, with my Seattle City Council campaign. Unfortunately, on August 6, the date of the primaries, I was not elected. I was hoping to win because it would lay out my path for the next four years, the term for a city council person. I've always been interested in politics because it's one of the few ways you can make a lasting social and community difference. I enjoy being a voice for our community.

In January 2019, I established Your Gift of Life Foundation. That's where my true love lies at the moment—in using my real-life experience to help others going through a similar situation. I'd like to travel all over the country, and internationally even, speaking to students and the younger generation, including sports teams, to let them know there is a way out of the darkest places if they hang in there, reach out for help, and keep working diligently. That's where my real joy lies—in helping to change and save lives on a more personal basis.

So where do I go from here? I've thought about that often. Now that I don't have any family, or business here in Seattle, and will likely lose my house, I really don't have much to hang onto in Seattle other than a bunch of dear friends. Seattle is still one of the most beautiful places in the world, but it's getting awfully expensive. I can't afford to stay here unless I really start putting things together again quickly. I do realize I have a lot of marketable skills, something I didn't realize when I was going through my dark period.

When I lost the Seattle City Council race, I considered just picking up and moving to China. I could then work a lot more closely with my colleagues there on study abroad programs and basketball training featuring a lot of former NBA players. I've been on my own for the last three years, and now that I'm in my early sixties, I don't want to face retirement alone. I want to continue traveling the world while still physically able to do so. I want to get out there and rebuild my retirement nest egg so I can look forward to my golden years.

You can ask yourself the same thing: "Where do I go from here?" There's no hurry, but after you get everything back in place and you're feeling healthy and like your old self again, you'll probably emerge out of that darkness with a whole new landscape of things to look at. Maybe you have experienced a lot of major changes like I did. The death of a loved one, a divorce, financial ruin, having to pick up and move to another location, health changes—there are a million things that can change your outlook on life, but you have to be prepared for it. All the years I ran the Donaldson Clinic, I used to keep a sign on my office wall that said, "Change Is Inevitable, But Growth Is Optional." Every time I looked at that sign, and every time I think of that quote, I remind myself that I choose to grow, no matter what the change.

Going through adversity will change you. It's up to you to grow with that change. You can do it.

QUESTIONS FOR REFLECTION

Make a list of changes you have recently experienced, such as in the last year or whenever you began to experience difficulties.

_____

_____

_____

_____

_____

_____

_____

_____

_____

_____

_____

_____

_____

What have you learned from these experiences? What growth have you experienced?

_____

_____

_____

_____

_____

_____

If you could begin today to live the life you want, what would that life look like? Be specific.

_____

_____

_____

_____

_____

_____

_____

Chapter 14

I'M SO GLAD I DIDN'T SNEEZE

I came up with the title of this chapter, based on one of my favorite sermons by Dr. Martin Luther King, Jr. In it, King describes a mentally deranged "Negro" woman who approached him during a book signing. Suddenly, the woman lunged forward at King and thrust a four-inch knife blade into his chest. Dr. King had to undergo life-saving emergency surgery. His doctors discovered the knife blade had come within a quarter-inch of severing his aortic artery. If that had happened, he would have bled to death on the spot within minutes. His surgical procedure was also so delicate that his doctors told him, if he would have sneezed, he surely would have died. As Dr. King recovered in the hospital, he received thousands of cards and letters from well-wishers. One letter was from a young white girl who wrote that she was so glad he hadn't sneezed.

These words from Dr. King's sermon reminded me of how precious life is. Sometimes, life happens to us; other times, we make life happen. Life constantly shows us over and over how little control we actually have. Yet, we do have the freedom to choose to do just about anything we'd like to do.

When my life seemed to be hanging on that thin line between "Should I stay and keep on living?" or "Should I end my life?" I ultimately chose to stay and keep on living.

What would sneezing have looked like?

- ☐ Sneezing would have been acting upon my impulses.
- ☐ Sneezing would have been following through with one of my plans to kill myself.

Believe me, there were numerous times when I wanted to "sneeze" so life would be over. But I'm so glad I didn't sneeze!

QUESTIONS FOR REFLECTION

When have you been tempted to "sneeze" (kill yourself or just let things fall apart) and didn't?

_____

_____

_____

What would have happened if you had sneezed?

_____

_____

_____

What good things have happened to you because you decided not to sneeze?

_____

_____

_____

Chapter 15

I'M NOT A VICTIM

As a person of color, an African-American man, I've lived my life with oppression, prejudice, racism, and not being given an equal opportunity. But I learned early on not to let any of those obstacles turn me into a victim.

Society is full of obstacles that can easily have one thinking they are victim of the circumstances. Yes, it's true you may have been held back or not given an opportunity, or it may be flat out racism and prejudice against you. But we have to do our best to overcome those situations and not become a victim of them. We can and we will overcome if we just keep on persevering and not give up.

The year 2020 was filled with all kinds of social and racial unrest. All of us were hurting from the pandemic that affected each and every one of us. A lot of us lost our jobs, and those jobs may never come back. Schools were shut down, and children had to resort to online learning. Our daily routines were disrupted as we had to resort to social distancing and wearing masks. Life as we know it may not return to "normal" until an actual vaccine is developed and distributed throughout the United States. Even then, we will all have to deal with a "new normal."

Sometimes, life just has a way of throwing you a curveball, and even though you may take a swing and miss, the important thing is never to give up.

Now, some people are victims of criminal activities, and I fully recognize that. Many of those crimes that are perpetrated against a person are life-altering, and the victim's life will never be the same. Those who suffer that fate are actual "victims," and there's no two ways about it. My heart goes out for each and every one of them.

However, in today's society, I note that many people seem to think of themselves as victims or resort to playing the "victim card." I don't know what causes it, but it's become so easy to just blame someone else for our problems. It's understandable that when your whole world turns upside down, the last person you want to point a finger at is yourself. However, that mindset only exasperates the distress and despair that accompany mental health challenges.

If we think back to the four agreements I discussed in Chapter 12, we will realize we need to be accountable for our own role in our situation. No matter what happens, unless we are forced to do something against our will, upon close examination, we will find that we have a part to play in it.

Yes, there are legitimate times when we are a victim—when we are assaulted, raped, robbed, mugged, betrayed, cheated on, or physically, sexually, or emotionally abused, or other instances where people hurt us against our will. We likely had little control in these situations to stop the abusive behavior from happening. These are horrible situations and the people who experience them are victims in those moments. But once the abusive event is over, we can work toward recovery and no longer feeling like a victim.

Being in some of these situations might also lead us to mental health issues, including depression. That is completely understandable and a natural result of such a situation. However, the best path to good mental health is to try not to act like a victim. Rather than focusing on the situation and being a victim of it, we need to get appropriate professional help when going through adversities. If we develop the mindset that we will not be or remain a victim, we can make our lives improve much more quickly.

It would have been so easy to blame my problems on my ex-wife, on the banks that would no longer give me a business loan, on the NBRPA and the NBA, on my accountant for my IRS woes, etc. But as long as I am able and willing to shoulder my share of the blame, I can make my way through a difficult situation. Once you take responsibility for your part in a situation, you are no longer a victim. You actually are empowering yourself so you can then take action to improve the situation. And once you begin to take action, the situation does improve. It may not happen overnight, but even slow progress is better than no progress—no progress is what you get when you stay stuck in a victim mentality.

QUESTIONS FOR REFLECTION

Are you playing the victim in your current situation? Why? How does being a victim make you feel?

_____

_____

_____

_____

_____

_____

Take some time to list everyone who is in some way to blame for your situation, including yourself. Then next to your list award percentage points to the share of the blame each person is due. For example, if you had a fight with your mom, it might be Mom 70%, Me 30%. This will help you see your role in the situation and what you can change to make it better next time.

_____

_____

_____

_____

_____

_____

Now that you have taken responsibility for your share of the situation, list three actions you will take to improve it.

1. _____

2. _____

3. _____

Chapter 16

LEARNING NOT TO ACT NEEDY

When you are going through depression or other troubles, you want some sympathy and help from others, and it's important to reach out to them for help. However, it's easy at such times to give up your own power and expect someone else to solve all your problems. At such times, you can hurt yourself further by acting too needy and driving other people away. Unfortunately, I've been in that situation and had to learn how not to overdo it and give in to being needy.

In February 2018, at the NBA All Star weekend in Los Angeles, I had a meeting with two high level executives from the NBA. Both came to the NBRPA Board of Directors meeting, as they do annually. I purposely arrived a few minutes early, before the other board members arrived, to see if I could grab a few minutes alone with both visitors to share with them how desperate I was feeling.

Remember, this happened in the midst of dark period I was going through.

I arranged to sit next to both of them, and it was just us and one or two others in the room for about ten minutes. I showed one of the executives a slip of paper on which I had written three items:

- ☐ Anxiety
- ☐ Depression
- ☐ Suicidal Ideations

I was scared, and he could see I was scared. I didn't think I was going to make it through the weekend. The thought of a former NBA player (me) committing suicide during All Star weekend, with a worldwide, global audience, was all I could think of. I didn't want to be alone in my hotel room.

The conversation was mainly between me and one of the executives since the other executive was semi-engaged in another conversation and being pulled in several directions at once. The executive I was speaking to expressed concern for my state and shared a similar situation he had dealt with recently with another person going through the same thing.

He said he would relate our discussion to his colleague so they would rally whatever resources they could to help me.

During the board meeting, ironically, the topic arose of some of the work the NBA was starting to do to support current players with mental health issues. Earlier in the season, two current players, Kevin Love and DeMar DeRozan, had spoken up about the mental health challenges they were dealing with. The NBA realized mental health support was something the players really needed.

Being a retired player, I realized the NBA's primary concern was for its current players, not those already put out to pasture. However, I was glad to have the NBA's ear, if only for a moment. The executive I was speaking to realized how serious my situation was and told me to call him anytime I needed to talk to someone. Of course, I wore my welcome out quickly, since he is a very busy person, but I was desperate and scared.

He and I agreed to meet the next morning over coffee, which gave me the sense that he really cared. I told him I didn't feel good about being away from my home in Seattle and by myself in my hotel room because I was afraid I might do something to harm myself. I told him I would feel better if I went back to Seattle to a more comfortable environment, so I left Saturday morning. Normally, All Star Weekend begins on Thursday and goes through Sunday evening.

Once I got home, I pestered him over and over with phone calls. I needed him, or anyone from the NBA family, to help me in my desperate state. I kept hoping for a paid player appearance or some minimal part-time thing to help get me back on my feet. But nothing came of all of that.

I fell further into depression.

When I got back to Seattle, I finally had to pull the plug on my long-running business. (The decision was made for me by my business' creditors.) Poof! There went my income, my identity, and my sense of accomplishment...there went everything! I was hurting, and in a very bad place. My NBA contact quit taking my calls, and poof! There went my sense of NBA family support. I don't blame them. I was being overly needy. My point is when you have someone to support you, don't push them away with being overly needy. Plus, I had to understand the NBA has other concerns than my mental wellbeing. They are about making money and providing entertainment for the fans. It's not that they don't care, but that I can't expect them to change their mission for me. I had to learn to toughen up and take responsibility for my problems, not expect others to fix them for me.

I had to call all of my employees that weekend to tell them our business was closing and arrange to meet with them on Monday morning as we cleaned out our workplace. It was one of the hardest times I've ever been through. Of course, I couldn't let the employees know what was going on with me. I had always been the strong, fearless leader during the twenty-eight years we had all been together. So, with a stiff upper lip, I held it together somehow as I told them all how much I appreciated them and how truly sorry I was that it was all coming to an end. Wow! That was tough!

It was best I didn't act needy with my employees, though. Over time, as I've discussed earlier in this book, I learned how to build up a support group so I had several people to turn to and not one person to dump everything on and become overly needy with. People want to help you, but they also have their own lives and can't drop everything for you. Once you understand that and have realistic expectations about the kind of help you can get from people, you will have a better chance of recovering from depression and other obstacles to your wellbeing.

QUESTIONS FOR REFLECTION

When have you asked for help and not received it?

_____

_____

_____

How did that make you feel?

_____

_____

_____

What role did you play in preventing yourself from receiving help?

_____

_____

_____

What would you do differently in that situation today?

_____

_____

_____

Chapter 17

I'M SO GLAD I'M NOT AN ANGRY PERSON

After everything I've gone through, I'm so glad I'm not an angry person who can easily be pushed over the edge. I can see now how and why some people reach the point of picking up a gun and mowing down as many people as they possibly can. They're not crazy—they're angry! They've taken one body blow after another, over and over again, until it just becomes too much.

We've all seen the headlines far too often in this country, where someone, typically a male (and a Caucasian male at that), feels he's losing everything to "them" (whoever "them" is in his mind) and just explodes. He might have just lost his job (a tipping point), lost custody of his kids (a tipping point), been served divorce papers (a tipping point), experienced road rage once too often (a tipping point), been rejected by someone he is interested in (a tipping point), or been in an argument yet again (a tipping point). All of these scenarios and more are enough to put anyone over the edge if they just keep building and building and building.

Most of us have a release valve, by which we can let off steam in a healthy way, but when we can't let off steam in a healthy way, things boil over. We live in such a fast-paced world that we have to find time to rebalance and catch our breath.

I don't believe people are inherently evil—that they are sitting around plotting how to hurt other people. Sure, some may have a warped sense of reality, but that's a mental health issue that needs to be treated. Then, that warped sense of reality keeps getting fed by whatever environment they are immersed in (often through the internet), and they find themselves acting that out. But evil? Very, very few people are just pure evil.

I was never truly angry or disappointed with anyone while going through my ordeal. I never thought to hurt anyone but myself. I was upset and angry at myself—no one else.

QUESTIONS FOR REFLECTION

Have you ever lost your temper and regretted it later? What were the results of your anger?

_____

_____

_____

_____

_____

_____

List productive ways you can diffuse your anger when it arises.

_____

_____

_____

_____

_____

_____

_____

_____

_____

_____

_____

Chapter 18

TURNING THE PAGE

One thing I did to help myself through my depression was to start publicly raising awareness about mental health issues. One result was the following article about me by Art Thiel that ran in *The Athletic* on May 16, 2018.[2]

***

THE
ATHLETIC

Turning the Page After Struggles—16 Year NBA Vet James Donaldson Wants to Help Young Athletes Shed Mental Health Stigma

Prone upon an overmatched bed, 7-foot-2 James Donaldson was affixed with tubes and monitor patches when Lenny Wilkens walked into the room at Swedish Hospital's intensive care unit. The former Sonics star player and championship coach, who gave Donaldson his first pro basketball job in 1980, spawning a 16-year NBA career that included an All-Star Game selection, was shocked.

2 Reprinted with permission from The Athletic.

"He seemed to recognize me," Wilkens says, sounding a little shaken. "But he couldn't speak."

That was January 2015. Donaldson can speak now passionately, supplemented often by a dazzling smile that these days offers a fragile counterpoint to the melancholy.

At 60, he can do many things. There's one thing he can't do: Forget.

Eleven-and-a-half hours of emergency heart surgery was followed by a week in a medically induced coma to prevent swelling in the brain. He spent two months in intensive care, followed by more months of arduous physical and emotional rehab.

For a 35-year vegetarian—never a smoker, drinker or drugger—who stayed fit after his playing career ended in Europe in the late 1990s, his physical travail left him bewildered and despairing.

"At the time, the doctors said they were worried about paralysis, a vegetative state, strokes, all kinds of things," he says. "On that line between life and death, I was right there."

As Donaldson struggled to regain his physical vitality, other matters closed in.

By 2017, an IRS audit revealed he owed back taxes. A woman and her 9-year-old son, with whom he had a long-term relationship, walked away, with no further contact. His business, the Donaldson Clinic, a physical therapy practice begun in 1989 that grew to three Seattle-area locations, faltered. In February 2018, the original office in Mill Creek was shuttered.

Donaldson lives alone in a big house in Magnolia. Late last year, the "alone" part was getting to him.

"One thing after another," he says. "Around Thanksgiving, I was really having trouble sleeping through the night. I didn't want to face these things. When I'd wake up in the middle of the night, I'd have a lot of dark, scary, negative thoughts.

"Including suicide."

A man who seemed to have managed the perilous transition from the celebrity-athlete life to a productive civilian life— he even ran for mayor of Seattle in 2009, finishing fourth in an eight-candidate field with more than 8,000 votes—was on the precipice.

Late in 2017, after several days of disrupted sleep, Donaldson called his family doctor, thinking he would be prescribed sleep medication. Instead, the doctor asked hard questions about the severity of his depression and his suicidal thoughts.

"He pressed me, asking how I would do it," Donaldson says. He doesn't own a gun, nor does he have drugs or alcohol in the house. He did say that every time he drives into his garage, he sees exposed rafters and a coiled rope.

"Been there for years," Donaldson says. "I told him, 'I guess that's one way.' He told me, 'Because you came up with that, you have a problem. You really need to work with us, and

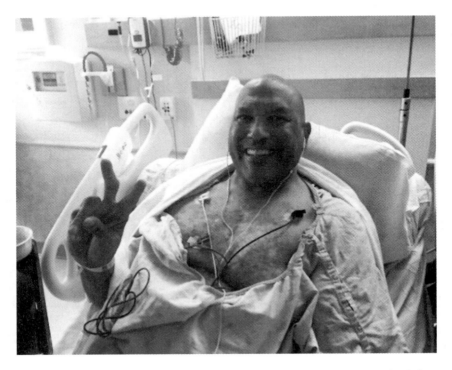

James Donaldson returned to Seattle's Swedish Hospital for a checkup in 2017. *(Photo courtesy James Donaldson)*

"He should have died that day."

An aortic dissection is a vascular disorder that occurs when the inner layer of the aorta, the large blood vessel branching off the heart, tears, and blood surges through the opening, causing the inner and middle layers of the aorta to separate, or dissect.

It's a rare condition, often genetic, and occurs a little more often in tall people. If it ruptures, death is usually swift.

As he met up at Seattle's Interbay golf course with friends for a round, he wasn't feeling right, even though he recently passed his annual physical exam. Sweaty, nauseous and experiencing sharp back pain, he excused himself from the group and managed to drive himself to his doctor's office at Ballard Swedish.

"I remember making it to his office, seeing the reception desk, and then everything went black," Donaldson says. "I don't remember anything thereafter for five or six days."

Dr. Peter Casterella is an interventional cardiologist (stents and angioplasty) at Swedish Hospital on Capitol Hill. He was on duty when Donaldson was wheeled into the operating room. His job was to get Donaldson's blood pressure under control.

"By all means, he should have died on the day it occurred," Casterella says.

Thanks to the swift, intense work by Dr. Samuel Youseff and the cardiology team at Swedish, Donaldson survived the aortic dissection. The physical recovery was slow—he was later diagnosed with sleep apnea—yet the psychological consequences are often harder to remedy.

"What happens to people who survive things like this, is there's a loss of part of themselves; they know they'll never be the same again," Casterella says. "There's a tremendous sense of guilt: 'I should be grateful for all these people who helped me, but all I feel is sad and depressed. And I feel guilty about that.'

"It's very normal for people who survive a life-threatening illness. This is part of what happens to people who adjust to what the consequences are."

Apart from health matters, other consequences kept piling up in his mind. While bedridden, Donaldson talked about what he called a "premonition." Casterella said it was a not unusual reaction to a near-death experience.

Donaldson described a mental image that had him looking down at himself as he flipped through pages of a photograph album.

"I'm looking at all the great things I'd done in my life to that point—friends, family activities," he says. "Then I turn the page, and it's totally black. At that point, I knew I was gone. I knew I wasn't going to make it."

Donaldson said he heard a voice he chose to call God's. The voice told him to have faith and turn the next page. He did. The page was black.

"So I'm starting to argue with God," he says. "I'm saying, 'Wait a minute. I've taken care of myself. I've always tried to do the right things. I'm only 57. What happened? I thought I'd be 85 or 95. My dad is 92 and still going.'

"God said, 'James, I told you, have faith. Turn the page.' I turned it. It, too, was black. I knew I was gone then."

Donaldson paused, teared up, and resumed his story.

"It was so real. I was fighting, and at the same time I was at peace. If God was calling me away, I was totally OK with that. But I was fighting.

"Again, I heard God's voice: 'I told you, James, have faith. Turn the other page.' I didn't want to do it, you know? But somehow, I turned the next page. It, too, was black.

"But after a few seconds, some faint images started appearing. Pictures of me, of friends.... It started becoming more vibrant, real. Like regular photos. I knew at that point I'd be OK.

"That was a tough thing. Real tough.'"

Some help from his friends

Quarterback Jack Thompson was a freshman at Washington State in the fall of 1976 when another freshman—"so tall and soooo skinny"—walked into the Cougars weight room after a prep hoops career in Sacramento.

"I remember thinking, (coach) George Raveling must see a lot in this guy," says Thompson, who as the "Throwin' Samoan" became one of the greatest sports figures in WSU history. "But skinny as he was, nobody outworked James Donaldson.

"By the time I left Pullman, he had totally changed his physique. When I saw him in the NBA, I said, 'Wow.' He made himself indispensable."

Circumstances now force upon Donaldson another transformation. He's had to learn to reach out and ask for help, a tough chore for many men who pride themselves on self-reliance.

Raveling, the bombastic Cougars hoops coach from 1972 to 1983, who later coached at Iowa and USC before becoming a global marketing director for Nike, predicted the change won't be easy.

"James by nature was not a gregarious person," says Raveling, 80, by phone from his Los Angeles home. "Even when he played for me he was an introvert, tending to keep things to himself.

"James has always had a wealth of potential … and his intellectual skills are much richer than he realizes. He quickly understood what he didn't know and was coachable, teachable and a hard worker. Those are three fundamental skills that escalate growth.

"Now he needs to remember those things and reinvent himself."

Raveling, Thompson and Wilkens are in a circle of people Donaldson has connected with in an effort to help him navigate the setbacks following the surgery.

"It saddens me to see what's happened," Thompson says. "He's one of the more cerebral athletes I've been around. Yet he had a string of things happen to him, and he mentioned his thoughts about suicide.

"When we last spoke, he was heading in a different direction and said he had a better handle on things. He values his friendships, and it's important that we be there for him."

Under a doctor's care, and with anti-anxiety medications, Donaldson's enlistment of friends made a difference over the holidays.

"Even though I'm not gregarious, I've always treasured friendships," he says. "It was natural for me to reach out to them for more than surface talks. I turned to them and the medical professionals, and they were there for me.

"They asked what they can do. I said, 'Maybe you could just call occasionally and check in on me. I live a life where people call on me wanting something. How about just calling me and seeing how my day is going? Check in to make sure I'm not going through anything too heavy.'

"They've all responded: 'We'll be there, even at two in the morning.' I was sending out distress text messages, obviously crying out for help. That helped me get through. My friends made me realize they will miss me.

"When I was in the midst of that, I really did not think anyone would miss me."

After the holidays, another test for Donaldson: the Jan. 16 suicide of Washington State junior quarterback Tyler Hilinski.

The inexplicable hits home

Shock over the death of a popular 21-year-old seemingly at the apex of college life still lingers in the Palouse, partly because the motives behind self-inflicted gunshot were neither foreseen, nor subsequently explained. Mental health issues can be diabolical that way.

Even though he never met his fellow Coug almost two generations younger, Donaldson had no shortage of empathy.

"I was feeling better, but Tyler's situation brought back some things," he says. "I was just imagining a 21-year-old with so much ahead of him, and I'm in the fourth quarter. He thought he had no one to talk to.

"It's a lot of pressure. Friends and family think he's a big star. Who understands that better than a former athlete?"

Hilinski was set to succeed Luke Falk, the Pac-12 Conference's all-time passing leader, in the fall. The two were close. Falk echoed Donaldson's sentiments when he met reporters at the Senior Bowl in Mobile, Ala.

"At times, we feel like we can't express our emotions because we're in a masculine sport," Falk says. "Him being the quarterback, people look up to you as a leader and so he felt, probably, that he really couldn't talk to anybody.

"So we've gotta change some of that stuff. We've gotta have resources and not have any more stigma about people going to them."

The seemingly inexplicable suicide of a burgeoning college football star is part of a growing nationwide conversation about mental health among athletes. Even if it seems less so to some fans, athletes are no less susceptible to problems.

"People look at athletes and entertainers on the outside as having it all together," Donaldson says. "On the inside, we can be as torn up as the next guy, or worse."

As much as colleges and pro sports franchises invest in the physical welfare of athletes, there is not the same commitment to psychological well-being, especially at a young age. Sports, it seems, are so much about the here and now.

"Most college and pro athletes don't have a personal development strategy," Raveling says. "They walk suddenly into a life full of money and people tugging on them. They put all their energy into the present, not the future. Many don't think of the future, and of their mental well-being."

But the social taboo, especially among men, against open discussion of mental health, seems to be changing.

In the middle of a personal-best season, Raptors forward DeMar DeRozan told the *Toronto Star* that he has been dealing for years with depression.

More intimately and expansively, another NBA All-Star, Kevin Love of the Cleveland Cavaliers, wrote a first-person essay on The Players' Tribune. Love chronicled a panic attack he had during a Nov. 5 game. He described his bewilderment, his reluctance to seek counseling, then positive results after a successful series of sessions with a mental health therapist.

"If you're suffering silently like I was, then you know how it can feel like nobody really gets it," he wrote. "Partly, I want to do it for me, but mostly, I want to do it because people don't talk about mental health enough. And men and boys are probably the farthest behind.

"I know it from experience. Growing up, you figure out really quickly how a boy is supposed to act. You learn what it takes to 'be a man.' It's like a playbook: Be strong. Don't talk about your feelings. Get through it on your own. So for 29 years of my life, I followed that playbook."

Earlier this month, another Players' Tribune first-person came from 13-year NBA veteran Keyon Dooling, who told of a trigger moment in a Seattle restaurant that evoked the horror of sexual abuse he experienced as a 7-year-old but kept hidden throughout his adult life.

James Donaldson began his pro career in 1980 at the Seattle Coliseum, now KeyArena. *(Photo credit: Alan Chitlik/Sportspress Northwest)*

A way forward

The morning after learning of Hilinski's suicide, Donaldson woke with an urge to tell the story of his own struggle with depression and suicidal thoughts. He wanted to help re-write the playbook Love mentioned.

"Something was tugging at me," he says. "Tyler can't tell his story, and telling his story is nothing I want to try to do. But his death motivated me to make sure my support was around me—friends, doctors, medications—everything I needed to fight back from a very dark place."

A longtime member of Mount Zion Baptist Church in Seattle's Central District, Donaldson recalled the words of Rev. Dr. Samuel B. McKinney, who pastored the church for 43 years until his death April 7.

"I remember him saying, 'Even if you think you've gone through life mostly problem-free with few challenges, just keep on living,'" Donaldson says. "Sooner or later, something will hit you—part of the great challenge of a long life. He lived a great one, but at the end he was 91 and in a wheelchair, housebound.

"We all will face issues that are mentally devastating."

Donaldson has found reward in purposefully sharing his story among people he knows best: athletes, whom he also knows are among the least likely to seek help.

In February, he was re-elected to a three-year term as a member of the board of directors of the NBA Retired Players Association, where he is pursuing mental health initiatives with the NBA.

He also is CEO of a startup business called Athletes Playbook, a mentorship program made up of veteran athletes helping younger ones. Focusing on scholarships, life mentoring and degree completion, the website says, "Our community of former professional athletes will provide a playbook for athletes, parents and coaches for high achievement in sports and life."

The subscription-based business seeks to develop connections with students, coaches, high schools and colleges that need help reaching athletes reluctant to talk about their anxieties as well as their aspirations.

The concept has led to conversations with athletic department officials at Washington State and the University of Washington about creating a non-clinical program to help break down the isolation some athletes feel in big-time programs.

"Mental health for student-athletes is my new advocacy," he says. We're trying to find out what a program looks like, and try to create a model. The long-term hope is to do it with more schools."

The discussion and the potential ways to help have done wonders for Donaldson's own outlook.

"I've gone from a place of hopelessness and despair to a place of hope," he says. "It's night and day. There are opportunities ahead. I'm striving for things, making new friends. I have a reason to get up and live. A few months ago, I had none of that."

He intends to be honest with young athletes. Progress, he will say, is often not steady. For older athletes he meets via the Retired Players Association, he is also honest about managing later-life stages, when body and mind don't respond as they once did.

Donaldson was hospitalized last week for a heart irregularity. His medications were adjusted, and he is back home, ever more mindful.

"Most of my days are good, but there's the occasional one…" he says. "On a recent Friday, on the end of a long week, I was exhausted. I suddenly wanted to end it all. How I keep reverting to that, I don't know. I still have a little sense of impending doom.

"We know to expect the physical changes. But managing the mental part of the changes is a hard thing. That is where I hope to help."

Donaldson doesn't have all the answers, but he's joined those who are breaking through the shame surrounding mental health in sports. He is no longer alone. With help, he keeps turning the page.

Art Thiel was a longtime sports columnist at the late *Post-Intelligencer* in Seattle. He co-founded Sportspress Northwest, a digital daily news and commentary site that chronicles the Seahawks, Mariners, Sounders and University of Washington sports. He recalls when George Karl and Gary Payton stopped arguing long enough to produce splendid springs of playoff basketball. Follow him on Twitter @Art_Thiel.

(Top photo: Nancy Hogue/Sporting News via Getty Images.)

THE ATHLETIC

QUESTIONS FOR REFLECTION

Do you believe it's true from your experience that "Everyone is going through something"?

_____

_____

_____

If so, how can that understanding change how you treat other people? Will you be more compassionate, take more time to really get to know people, etc.?

_____

_____

_____

Chapter 19

WILL SUICIDE ALWAYS BE AN OPTION?

Previously, I mentioned my conversation with my friend, Chuck Wright, a mental health professional. I asked him, "Will suicide always be an option?"

After continuing to work my way through all my mental challenges, I can emphatically say, "Hell, yes!"

Chuck told me the same thing. He said after going through everything I've been through, and the challenges so many people who deal with mental health challenges go through, yes, suicide will always (unfortunately) be an option for me and them.

Actually, it's an option for all of us, whether we are dealing with mental health issues or not, but when you're dealing with mental health issues, it has a way of making the top of your list of options for dealing with whatever you're going through.

I said this before, but it bears repeating. Suicide as an option works like this: If you are mentally healthy and you have a list of options, maybe the top twenty-five ways you deal with challenges, suicide will typically be at the bottom of the list. But when you go through mental health challenges like I and so many others have gone through, suicide tends to work its way up into the top ten options, and if you continue to struggle and not seek help, it easily moves up into the top five, and then, if you continue to struggle without getting help, it can become all-consuming—becoming the only option on your list.

I still find that the suicide option raises its ugly head from time to time when I'm under serious stress or I get hit by another big life event that seems to be too much to bear.

After things started settling down for me, toward the end of 2019, when my home, which I had lived in for almost forty years, ended up in foreclosure, I was forced to move out within forty-five days, which was a big challenge for me physically. Living on limited funds, I couldn't afford to hire a moving company.

All of the heaviness came back and the suicide option started to move up the list. It even got to the point where, instead of having to go through the ordeal of uprooting my life, I almost convinced myself it would be better if someone just found my body. I know it's a hideous thought, but when you are in that frame of mind, those are the thoughts you have.

I've told my friends that I feel like I am of two minds all the time. One is my rational and logical mind, where I mentally spend about 95 percent of my time. But once in a while, my irrational and illogical mind pops up, and I begin thinking about giving up. That's the push and pull tug-of-war that goes on inside people dealing with mental challenges. You would think with a 95:5 ratio it would be easy to win every time. But that 5 percent is a very powerful and impulsive voice that continues talking to you, trying to convince you to do things you will forever regret.

So far, I'm continuing to plug away and make some good headway on my journey to complete mental health, but I guess the experiences I've gone through have scarred me for life, so suicide is something I will remain aware of at all times—and it may come back to haunt me.

My advice to anyone going through a similar situation is to realize you do have those two voices inside your mind. Make sure you listen to the rational and logical voice and not the other one. Eventually, your healthy mind will win out and keep you in a good place.

QUESTIONS FOR REFLECTION

If you have thought about suicide, list all the rational reasons why it is not the best option.

If you have not already done so, reach out for help now. A good place to begin is the National Suicide Prevention Lifeline. I challenge you to call it now and begin to get the help you need:

NATIONAL SUICIDE PREVENTION LIFELINE
1-800-273-8255

Chapter 20

I AM NOT A VICTIM, AND NEITHER ARE YOU

I talked about being a victim back in Chapter 15, but as I wrap up this book, I want to emphasize this point one more time: try not to feel like a victim. Life has its trials and tribulations (and if you are a Christian like me, there are many Bible verses that can help and comfort you during them), and it's going to be full of ups and downs, good days and bad days. The important thing to remember is *you are not a victim.*

That's the approach I took throughout my ordeal. I realized sometimes life just happens, and there is really nothing we can do about it other than just try to endure. Short of someone tying you up and gagging you, almost every situation you get into comes from your own free will and your own choices. We are all going to face things like health issues, financial issues, maybe divorce, the death of a loved one, betrayal by a close friend, disappointment, etc. In all of those things, we have a part to play.

We have to realize that loved ones will pass on. Most likely, it will be our parents and older relatives, and then as we get older, it will be some of our peers; possibly, the very unfortunate situation may happen where we lose one of our own children. All of those things are likely to send us into a tail-spin we may find difficult to get out of, but we have to realize those are just things that happen along our journey of life, and even though we feel like it happens only to us, in reality, it happens to everyone.

When you find yourself in that deep, dark place of mental challenges, try not to lash out at others out of frustration or anger. Please realize that anger is a sign of depression and a sign that you need to get help. Make sure you reach out to medical professionals to get some help—appropriate pre-scription medications, mental health counseling—and be sure to bring together your small group of intimate friends. All of these things will help keep you balanced and help you realize you are not alone in this battle.

QUESTIONS FOR REFLECTION

What advice in this book have you not chosen to follow so far?

_____

_____

_____

_____

_____

_____

What is keeping you from following through?

_____

_____

_____

Are your reasons for not seeking the help you need legitimate?

_____

_____

_____

Are you being honest with yourself?

_____

_____

_____

Chapter 21

HOW DO YOU KNOW WHEN YOU'VE HIT ROCK BOTTOM...AND DOES IT MATTER?

After all I went through, I kept wondering when I would hit rock bottom, and I thought rock bottom would be when I lost my home.

My fight to save my home went on for more than a year—I lost.

All the time my house was in foreclosure, I had two options:

1. Get someone to lend me about $80,000 so I could make up all of the missed payments. Then the mortgage company would pull the house out of foreclosure, and I could pick up where I left off with monthly payments.
2. "Short sale" my house, meaning I would sell it for less than I owed and all the debtors would agree to settle for less. That could be very difficult because there were three liens on the house besides the original mortgage.

I ended up feeling stuck for more than twelve months.

Then, to start off 2020, within the first five weeks, three big life-altering events hit me—bam, bam, bam, one after another.

The first was that I filed for Chapter 7 bankruptcy. That would finally get all of my creditors off my back—a good $800,000 worth.

I don't feel bad about that at all. My bankruptcy attorney has been working with me to put together a strategy for moving forward. He removed all the scariness and stigma of bankruptcy for me by simply breaking it down in a way that made me realize it's a strategy many people have used over the years so they can get their financial lives back together, and that's exactly what it's there for.

The second thing that happened in early 2020 was that my house was finally put up for auction. There was no stopping it and no turning back. That was a big shoe that dropped because I had lived there for nearly forty years. Of course, it was difficult to deal with having all of that information publicly filed, and to have people calling me out of the woodwork to see if they could help me through the situation (mainly to their benefit).

The third thing that dropped on me was during the first week of February, when I underwent another major surgery, this time on my diaphragm and lower right lung. It was serious, and I was hospitalized for eight days, plus slowed down for the next eight weeks. It was something that needed to be done, because for a year, I had been experiencing increasing shortness of breath and great fatigue with the slightest exertion.

How's that for starting off the new decade? Not to mention the pandemic that hit all of us.

But you know what? Each time one of those things hit me, sure, I was rattled and startled, and it was like a sucker punch to the gut, but I kept my wits about me. I took a deep breath and realized it wasn't the end of the world and I'm still here.

It's not the end of the world until it's actually the end of the world. That is the essence of this whole book.

It will only be the end of the world for you if you pull the plug on your own life, and that's the last thing I or anybody else would want you to do.

When you feel like you can't get any lower, just find a way to step back from the situation, take a deep breath, realize you're still alive, and it's not the end of the world. There are ways to work out virtually every situation if you just approach it strategically and don't play the victim card, acting totally helpless.

So, here I am in early 2020. I look at myself and I think, *I have actually lost everything.* Everything I have worked so hard for over the last forty-some years, including my health. But one thing I still have is my life to live.

I'm still more fortunate than many. I'm not homeless and living in a tent under the bridge by the freeway (whether by choice or not). Sure, I'll have to vacate the house I'm living in in a few weeks and move into an apartment, but that beats being out on the streets. I don't even own my car since I'm obligated to make monthly payments. Most of my personal belongings (clothes, office equipment, computers, and the like) are all paid off, so they actually belong to me. But other than that, I'm walking away from this home I've lived in most of my adult life in a car that I don't fully own, with a lot of personal belongings I actually own. And my health is still iffy at best.

But when I look at my situation, I realize I am still more fortunate than most. My mind is still sharp and keen. I can think. I can visualize. I can dream. And most importantly, I have hope that tomorrow will be a better day. That, in itself, motivates me to keep going.

I know I can make it, even though I'm starting from scratch all over again. I have come down from the heights I achieved throughout my life as a professional athlete, college graduate, business owner, and so many more things, to the depths of where I am now. All that is okay because I still have what it takes to pick myself up, dust myself off, and keep on going—and I will.

These are the things I want you to keep in mind as well.

Unless you are incarcerated, no one is physically holding you back against your will from getting out there and doing what you need to do. If you need to get back to school, you should do it. If you want to start a business, plenty of mentors are out there who can get you started and be with you along that journey. If you want to become a homeowner, it doesn't take much more than a down payment and a decent credit rating, and there are a lot of tools and resources available to help you.

Here I am, remaking myself for the umpteenth time, and that's okay. I know I can do it. My health will continue improving as time goes on, and that's a good thing. And I'm looking forward to putting a wonderful family back together again so I can work on rebuilding my nest egg and roll into my retirement years.

I've come a long way from where my downward spiral began five years ago. Going through all of the physical, financial, mental, family, and relationship challenges I experienced and still being here to tell the story is remarkable in itself.

When I finally started coming out of the darkness, and was able to begin regaining my footing, what I most wanted to do was become an advocate for mental health awareness and suicide prevention. I hope I've helped you, whether or not you've gone through tragic and challenging experiences. I also hope my helping you will encourage you to help others.

My old pastor used to say we are in one of three phases at all times—like an eagle flying high in the sky, we are either flying into a storm, in the midst of the storm, or exiting the storm (a little tattered and beaten, but ready to do it all over again). No one knows how long those nice, calm periods before the storm will last. They might be decades for some of us, or they might just be a matter of a few weeks. We can't predict it; all we can do is realize storms are part of life's journey.

There will be ups and downs, trials and tribulations, but with a good head on your shoulders, good people around you, and medical professionals at the ready, you can get through anything life has to throw at you.

I want you to get out there and live life to its fullest, because after all, life is meant to be lived, and to be lived abundantly.

FINAL THOUGHTS

Thank you for taking the time to read about my personal experiences of going through that very dark and depressive state of my life, in which I almost ended up taking my life.

Suicide and depression are very difficult topics to talk about. Not many people are comfortable opening up and talking about their own thoughts, or even listening to other folks who had those kinds of thoughts.

The reason I have shared my story with you is I feel like I fall into the category of people who have had "suicidal ideations" but didn't followed through on it, rather than as someone who actually attempted suicide. Believe me, the thoughts were so real, and my plans were so well thought out, but I never did attempt to take my life. And I'm so glad I didn't.

Sometimes, life has a way of just "piling on." Right when you're just about ready to get to your feet, you get waylaid by another crushing blow.

Heck, 2020 alone started out with me filing for bankruptcy, having my home foreclosed on, and losing it in a "short sale," and another major surgery that sidelined me for the first two months of the year. And, of course, it was followed by the COVID-19 pandemic that affected all of us.

As I detail in my story, my difficulties were pertaining to my health and major surgeries, finances, personal relationships, and feeling that certain groups and individuals that I really put my trust and faith into betrayed me and disappeared on me, just when I needed them most.

You might be dealing with certain problems such as family issues or issues with close friends, spouses, or exes, or children, or with job, finances, or health issues. Everyone's situation is going to be different. I don't share my stories just to show you what I went through, I share my stories so you can relate what I went through with whatever you're going through. And I share so you can know that there is a way to work your way through all of that.

And here I am, a couple of years past the darkest point in my life, and for the most part—I'd say about 98 percent of the time—I feel really upbeat and positive about life and all it has to offer. But there are still another couple of percentage points that pop up from time to time and cause me to doubt if life is worth living. I quickly shake myself out of that mindset and focus on the positive rather than the little negative things that try to trip me up from time to time.

I don't want any of us to think of ourselves as "victims." Yes, there are actual times when we are victimized by a perpetrator, and that can bring on tremendous mental anguish in itself. But, personally, I think what most of us go through in dealing with mental issues are things that continually don't seem to go our way, and especially when they pile on top of each other, it makes us feel like maybe the world will be better without us.

I don't want any of us to think that way because we all have so much still to contribute to this world.

When I look around me now, and I see all of the thousands and thousands of people whose lives I have touched in a positive way, I realize that I do have tremendous value. I did back then and even now.

Be kind to yourself. Love yourself. Be good to yourself.

Your life is meant to be lived, and to be lived abundantly.

James Donaldson

James Donaldson

ABOUT THE AUTHOR

James Donaldson completed a twenty-year professional basketball career in the spring of 2000. He established The Donaldson Clinic in January 1990 shortly after a career-threatening knee injury with an idea that he would eventually become a physical therapist. He operated the Donaldson Clinic until 2018. He is a strong advocate for women- and minority-owned businesses and is very involved with various chambers of commerce. He understands what it takes to sustain a strong business environment that is conducive to the success of businesses overall.

James is a Washington State University graduate ('79). After an outstanding basketball career with WSU, he went on to play professional basketball in the NBA with the Seattle Supersonics, San Diego/L.A. Clippers, Dallas Mavericks, New York Knicks, and Utah Jazz. He also played for several teams in Spain, Italy, and Greece as part of the European Leagues, plus he toured with The Harlem Globetrotters to wrap up his career. James was an NBA All-Star in 1988 while playing center for the Dallas Mavericks. In 2006, James was inducted into the Pac-10 Sports Hall of Fame and also the Washington State University Athletic Hall of Fame.

Today, James devotes the majority of his time to various community activities and toward The Gift of Life Foundation (www.YourGiftOfLife.org), speaking on mental health awareness and suicide prevention.

James frequently conducts speaking engagements (motivational, inspirational, educational) for organizations, schools, and youth groups. He is the author of *Standing Above the Crowd* (www.StandingAboveTheCrowd.com).

A longtime resident of Seattle, in 2009, James was a candidate for mayor. He had a strong fourth place finish in a crowded field of eight candidates. In 2019, he was a candidate for Seattle City Council—District 7. He continues to work closely with several elected officials in regards to politics, youth, and educational issues in Seattle.

James believes in being a role model of success and professionalism for the scores of young people he devotes so much of his time to. He currently serves on several boards and/or committees and is a member of many organizations.

James believes in developing relationships that create a "win-win" environment for everyone involved, and being the best he can be!

BOOK JAMES DONALDSON TO SPEAK AT YOUR NEXT EVENT

Contact James to speak to your group or organization.
His main audiences typically consist of:

Youth groups and students

Current and former athletes

Men's groups and their significant others

Contact James at:

jamesd@yourgiftoflife.org

www.YourGiftOfLife.org

800-745-3161 (fax and voicemail)

Your Gift of Life

c/o James Donaldson

3213 W. Wheeler St. #162

Seattle, WA 98199